Once Upon a Blue Moon

MEMOIRS OF A WOMAN IN THE MIDDLE OF HER LIFE

{
*An Accidental Tour Guide to
Surviving Mid-Life Singlehood,
Reclaiming the Self, Redesigning Happiness
and Giving Love Another Chance*
}

BY TAMYRA BOURGEOIS, PH.D

Tamyra Bourgeois, Ph.D
Once Upon a Blue Moon
Baton Rouge, Louisiana
298 pages / ISBN 978-0-615-56203-2

Cover Illustration Brent Bourgeois
Photograph Vince Hayward
Graphic Design Chanler Holden

Also published by Tamyra Bourgeois:
How to Raise Happy, Loving Emotionally Intelligent Kids

MEMOIRS OF A WOMAN IN THE MIDDLE OF HER LIFE

www.tamyra.com

DEDICATION

This book is dedicated to my fearlessly loving and courageous widowed-single mother. You also lost your love, my father, in the middle of your life, and in the process of your recovery taught me that life not only goes on, but that life as a middle aged woman can be shaped, shifted and designed into a rich, rewarding, amazing new adventure.

Though there were times I felt afraid Mom, I was never paralyzed by my fears. I stood strong because I watched you carefully in my impressionable young adult years and was imprinted with your grace and valor. It is my true hope that the reader will find that same inspiration in watching me reinvent happiness as well.

ONCE IN A BLUE MOON

December 31, 2009

Driving on New Year 's Eve to my hip, intimate New Thought church alone – ah, correction: Driving on New Year 's Eve to my hip, intimate New Thought church "with myself" – I catch the full to overflowing Blue Moon glaring at me from the left side of my Hummer.

If I were still a practicing Old Testament Christian, I might indulge a moment with that Old Testament God just insidious enough to hang it there to make me pay penance for all my trespasses against men. If I indulge the Yogi in me, I might think this Blue Moon was a karmic symbol of all the hearts I'd broken in my youth, and the energy of those heart-breaks, having chased me through time, finally catching up to me now. If I still believed in the great destroyer (as in the nemesis of the great creator), I would be certain Satan hung it there to destroy the solace I might have otherwise found on this beautiful moonlit holiday night.

In my car heading to send the old year off with good riddance, this full Blue Moon looms ominously over my left shoulder, mocking my desire for acceptance of what is. It's literally a glaring example of my losses this year. And in this moment, I'm feeling all of them ...yes, I'm feeling full to overflowing with Blue Moon Sadness, and I'm hoping the Native American drumming ceremony I'm about to attend will lift me out of despair and up into a sacred space of joyful celebration.

In the meantime, it doesn't escape my awareness — nor does it take all of my eight-plus years as a student of behavioral science — to notice a recurring Freudian slip. I continue to write a "d" instead of an "n" after "moo" — "mood" rather than "moon."

WHICH IS IT? REALLY? BLUE MOOD OR BLUE MOON?

Perhaps they're one in the same tonight.

As I continue to backspace and erase, I'm aware that the "d" and the "n" are one space down and four spaces across from each other on my keyboard, and a mere 240,000 miles between this Blue Moon and my aching heart tonight.

CHAPTER 1

SHOULD OLD ACQUAINTANCE
BE FORGOT?

Reflecting on this last day of a difficult but emotionally expansive year, 2009 brought the final curtain call to a war torn but passionate decade with my former spouse Ryan - a man so handsome he's hard to fully take in: An exotic cross between Johnny Depp and Antonio Banderas, and ever so metro-sexy that he can wears jeans and a t-shirt with as much panache as he wears that knee weakening grey flannel suit.

His exquisitely elegant, wavy black hair –sometimes long, sometimes short, but always meticulously groomed – is his feature-feature. Equally dramatic are his perpetually penetrating sometimes grey, sometimes green eyes: eyes that won me over the very first time I had the great fortune and almost equal misfortune to trip and fall right into them; Eyes that in the first moment of their discovery, my breath literally came to a dead drop as my heart leaped right out of my chest into his hands. Since that fateful moment, not many days have gone by that we have not shared our love — as well as the projections of our painful childhood traumas — with and on each other.

Only now am I finally extracting my heart from the hard, firm grip of his own — his a heart that alternated between squeezing the life out of, and caressing the life back into mine. And yes, I let it happen - not intentionally, not fully unintentionally, no more a victim than a volunteer, but somehow I let it happen. For ten years we participated in the extreme sport of loving each other — riding the euphoric highs and being bludgeoned by the disastrous crashes of our differences. Some parts of me survived the crashes. Some parts of me did not. But the parts of me that are truly stronger in the broken places are willing, perhaps even compelled, to write about it now.

Like our relationship, or his sometimes long, sometimes short hair, he's a man full of inconsistencies. He's quick-witted when he is not in angst... full of light when he's not filled with the darkness of our collective despair. Yes, the only thing darker than his luscious hair was his mood — that is, his mood when he was with me. In the arms of his new lover, he seems to be lighter now. And ironically, or perhaps not, we share more exchanges of wit, playfulness, and forwarding conversation than ever before.

Despite our many difficulties together, he's forever endeared himself to me by way of fathering our beloved child. Gabriel came into existence on a marvelous and exquisitely rainy Gulf Coast Florida holiday night – as I alluded to above, and as was the case that weekend, the great was off-the-charts scorching, but the bad was so bad that it was below the threshold of sanity...the kind of relationship that left a heart torn and shredded straight through to the sub-atomic particles that lie below the deepest muscle...the place where the ache burned so badly that it literally caused my heart to malfunction with arrhythmic heart beats for almost two years.

Ours was the kind of relationship that begets the phrase, "When it's good it's great, but when it's bad, it's horrible" – the kind of relationship no one wants to leave, but in which few can stay. But in the end a part of me still wanted to stay. I loved him, and I loved the challenge. It is my nature to seek it, and I am tenacious in my efforts to negotiate with it.

CHAPTER 2

BOHEMIAN POET

Of course, to make matters worse, I dismiss my own advice to take a breath or two between lovers, and I tried to forget an old love with a new one. Which, incidentally, is advice I won't bother to give any longer – the breather part that is, and my apologies to all my friends and clients for giving it, because skipping that breather works! It works in the same way Vicodin works on a bad rotator cuff injury. The pain is still there, but with the introduction of the new chemicals, the ache fades into the background, as the bliss takes front row and center.

So out with the old and in with the new...a passionate bohemian poet nonetheless. This panacea worked for about a quarter of the year. It worked just long enough for Ryan to introduce a new woman into my life without me needing to slash her tires as a spousewarming gift. It did, however, finally rebound on itself, coming to a screeching halt at the beginning of the holiday season.

My bohemian poet was as handsome as my former spouse, but in a bit of a shabby chic sort of way – the kind of carelessly casual style that only a tall, dark and confidently handsome word-artist can pull off. Tall, dark, handsome, and way beyond ordinary in his intellect, Spencer has brown eyes as rich and creamy as expensive dark chocolate. My bohemian lover also had a flare for romance that could give Don Juan a really good run for his money. Thirty-six years of age, not thirty-two like my former spouse, but still a gap of many years between my birth and his own, his specialty I came to learn, was rescuing damsels in distress. And boy was he some kind of wonderful at it.

Our short, sweet, single-season, one-act play went something like this: Having just returned from a summer excursion in a foreign land teaching journalism to Thai students, he landed back in the States in late summer and quickly whisked me right out of my sensible shoes onto a plywood dance floor. For starters, an all-nighter in New Orleans beginning with my godson's Mixed Martial Arts fight, dancing the night away on Bourbon Street with bourbon on ice, and for dessert, a sunrise walk through the swamps of Jean Lafitte National Park.

Next came an enchanted Labor Day weekend camping trip that included a Zydeco festival in Plaisance, Louisiana. Zydeco is a delirious fusion of Cajun and Blues that keeps your feet stomping and your hips swaying all day and night long. We literally spent that season dancing together in smoky blues juke joints and quaint old listening venues that are typical of New Orleans and its surrounding parishes. When we weren't dancing, we were reading and writing poetry together and for each other—ahh... Whitman by the lake light of our own silvery moon, and sharing the smoldering love poems we wrote for each other. And one particular poem he wrote just for me, he read atop an old New Orleans balcony on my 50th birthday. The backdrop for this glorious poetry reading: a gorgeous old bed and breakfast called The Degas House overlooking Esplanade, which is arguably the most beautiful street in New Orleans.

And then, upon returning with my bohemian lover from San Francisco—the second most romantically productive Thanksgiving weekend I've spent (see Florida trip above)—our flaming, ultra-steamy cool relationship dropped abruptly off the edge of my life's continental shelf and took a dramatic dive into the eternal slope of darkness. The outer reasons for this sudden shift are between the two of us, as my reverence for him and his life choices demand my confidentiality here.

Truthfully, I'm staring up at that full, blue moon, with a double heartache tonight. There's a stabbing, momentary wondering of with whom he might be sharing his full, blue New Year's moon kiss. However, the greater genesis of my stabbing full moon pain is centered around my beloved spouse of the last decade and his new love.

Unfortunately, I know with whom the father of my second son is sharing his full blue moon New Year's kiss: a woman, much to my ego's dismay, who is likable and kind. I've even tried to find something I don't like about her, but I can't. And this aggravates me.

She's a Catholic administrator nonetheless. This, from a man for whom my mother burned Our Lady of Guadalupe candles and said many Novenas to the Italian monk and recently canonized Saint Padre Pio. Yes, she prayed religiously and fervently for his con-

version to Catholicism, and though he has not con-
verted, his new relationship is more evidence,
I recently told her, that we really need to watch what
we pray for.

AND TWAIN WAS RIGHT:
TRUTH IS STRANGER THAN FICTION.

CHAPTER 3

MENOPAUSAL MADNESS

To make matters dramatically worse, I'm trying to process the double heartbreak of 2009 through the filter of my very own intensely hot, erratic, hormonal hurricane—otherwise known as Menopause. Menopause lives up to everything the few good women who have had the courage to talk or write honestly about it claimed.

For any woman who happens to be in the midst of it now, or any man, woman, child, co-worker or friend who come within a five mile radius of a woman in menopause, be forewarned, it is not just a phase of life, it's a temporary form of insanity.

It's interesting however, that all I ever heard about were the hot flashes. And this was not very useful information, considering I've been a resident of Southern Louisiana most of my life, and heat is something I know how to handle. The real problem here is the set of symptoms no-one seems to want to admit to having. The absolute erratic mood swings, the over-sensitivity to as much as a sideways glance, the delusional features that have us believe that we are justified in our tirades. Of course these delusions stem from the mother of all menopausal delusions which is the belief that nothing's wrong with us and everyone else turned into an asshole overnight.

Had I not had an honest office manager and a deeply honest relationship with my daughter Claire, I would have probably joined the ranks of the blindly delusional as well. Fortunately, over the last 20 years as a mental health professional, I've developed enough self-insight to accept feedback from loved ones after the hundredth time they told me I was "not acting like myself."

Sad part is that even though I believe them, even though I can often see my erratic behaviors in hindsight, when I'm in the midst of my delusional, over sensitive, no one cares about my well-being moments, as well as the mole-hill is definitely a mountain moments, I'm thoroughly convinced that I'm the only rational person in the room. Yes, delusional, and I'm smack dab in the middle of it now.

Truthfully it's not all bad. There's also a delusional up-side. The upside is like a weird sort of Ecstasy trip

(Now I feel compelled to note here that I have never tried Ecstasy, reason being: both schizophrenia and bipolar are familial, so I've thought it wise to save my remaining good brain cells just in case I might be a late bloomer for psychosis.) And though my family history of mental distress might be a deterrent to the use of psychedelic drugs, it doesn't preclude me from having a special voyeuristic interest in this drug—a drug so awe inspiring that it has the ability to dump copious amounts of endorphins in a very short amount of time, heightening sensual pleasure to the point of erotic delusion.

Admittedly, I have a strange sort of admiration for this drug, and have been an occasional guest in the experiences of those I know who do partake and are willing to talk about it. So from what I can gather the ecstatic delusional feature of menopause is very similar. I have the low delusions and the high delusions. In other words I'm living in a body that has no idea what to do without functioning reproductive organs as I am riding the big Kahuna waves right now, waxing and waning on the ultra highs and ultra lows. Everything glorious is gloriously intense, and funny, and joyful, and ridiculous...much like my clients in the manic phase of bipolar disorder—and yes, the ones on Ecstasy as well. But the lows, my lows, let's just say they prompted my daughter to warn me that if I didn't ask my doctor for hormone medication, she was going to have to start taking medication just to visit me.

The best way I can describe this phenomenon is to say that I feel like a middle-aged crazy lady has trespassed on my insides, parked her travel trailer in my lower three chakras, hung those fiesta lights around the carport, and taken up residence there. And since I love my family, I'm contemplating hormone replacement. At present, I'm weighing the pros and the cons. The biggest con right now is that hormonal sedation might just take the edge right off of my desire to blog this year's memoirs. Leaving things as they are now, I get the full hit of how far the crazy can take me and us as women, and I can document it here for the benefit of all...sort of like a home-based scientific study with my own junior science kit.

On the other hand, like Dr. Jekyll/Mr. Hyde or Bruce Banner and The Incredible Hulk, I fear my research project might just push me past the point of no return. This, I fear not quite as much as I fear being a coward for not toughing it out. So, not quite sure which direction to take yet, I'll continue to report from the trenches of hormonal madness. And as for the hot flashes - I've been spared by day but ambushed by night. Over and over again, like Count Dracula, they attack by moonlight. But when the sun shines in my window and I rise to greet the day with my T-shirt damp and clinging to my skin, I'm free of them again.

An educational piece here: the research I've done claims that the hot flashes occur when the blood sugar plummets, as in sleeping hours. The article suggested eating every two to three hours to prevent them. So I've contemplated buying one of those mini dorm fridges for my bedroom and setting my alarm to ring for a midnight, 2 a.m. and 4 a.m. snack. The fear that prevents me from doing this, however, is that I'm single again, which means I can afford the hot sweats way more than I can the calories.

As an alternative, I've gathered all the extra pillows in my home so that I have about six of them in bed at any time. It's winter, so I lower the temperature to 61 degrees and advise family members and house guests to wear sweaters and robes, sometimes both, to bed. When the hot flashes begin, I take the hot wet pillow from behind my head and in my half-sleep grab a fresh, 61 degree replacement to ice my neck back down again. In the end, it doesn't prevent the hot flashes, nor keep me sound asleep, but my pillow system does reduce the intensity of the flashes, as well as my desire for a midnight menopausal snack.

Sometimes in the middle of all the unpleasantries, either in the middle of one of my flashes or when I've disturbed those around me sufficiently enough to get feedback, I curse nature itself. Sometimes I grit my teeth and yell inside myself, "Alright then Mother Nature. I get it. Now that I can't reproduce for you anymore you have no use for me. Huh? You don't care, do you, if I go crazy and the tribe gets so sick of my mood swings that it takes me out into the deep woods and leaves me there to go crazy alone?"

Hot, delusional, erratic, hyper-sensitive and excessive – the dirty little secrets of Menopause. And as my dear mentor Andy Shurr once said; "Secrets keep us sick." So I'm letting the hormonal cat out of the bag right now. Ready?

As many of you near and dear to us women have

suspected, it's not you. It's us. We menopausal women are driving ourselves crazy and taking you along for the ride. And this too shall pass.

CHAPTER 4
NEW YEAR'S INTENTION

Driving on my Full Blue Moon New Year's Eve, boiling to overflowing with hormonal excesses and deficiencies, I ponder the possibility of meeting an attractive and interesting man this evening. I've been told by a mentor that I'm a meta-optimist, which means it's rare that I see even a completely empty glass as half-empty. And yes this is a curse as often as it is a blessing. So, true to form, I'm anticipating an outstanding evening with good friends and great rituals. And despite the fact that not once in the 10 years of attending my church have I met a single man I would consider dating, I optimistically (as in meta-optimistically) massage sexy smelling designer shampoo through my straight shoulder-length hair, while wondering if I might possibly break a 10-year streak and meet a charming churchman tonight that I let close enough to smell it.

Once there, leaving the Full Blue Moon outside in the cold to gloat alone, and stepping into the warmth and light of my beloved church, I did end up meeting a handsome older man. After a short deposition, I discovered he was attending my church for the second time. But even though I tried to stretch myself to find him of interest, I fixated on the wrinkles at the base of his ears and honed in on the occasional cracking of his aging voice, and thus his aging skin and voice became an impediment to the possibility of being attracted to him. I think he was about fifty-nine, eight or so years my senior. This age thing...ahhhh, I'm working on it. And, yes, I feel only a slight bit of shame in trying to evoke a pop-and-sizzle for this gentleman while standing in the reception area of my church—obviously not enough shame to prevent me from writing about it, or to prevent me from heading straight to the church bathroom, to make sure the lipstick I applied in the car, by the light of that despicably silvery Blue Moon, was in proper quantity and dimension.

Still optimistic and not wanting to waste a particularly good guy, I quickly text my best friend Sylvia (10 years my senior) with an urgent message: "ATTRACTIVE OLDER MEN HERE! REPEAT, ATTRACTIVE OLDER MEN!" Though she was already on her way to meet me, I do think that my warning raised her expectations a bit, and she walked in with an extra gorgeous stride to her already gorgeous Latin step. Having been self-assigned the role of her match-maker, I was disappointed to learn that she only found him "somewhat" attractive.

I, on the other hand, am mystified by why I found him attractive – but only in an "attractive-for-an-older-man" sort of way. I continue to wonder why, despite the fact that I find older men attractive, I don't find myself attracted to them. I want to. Truly, I want to, as I remember a friend's grandmother once saying: "Better to be an older man's darling, than a younger man's fool." And I've certainly been the latter—on more than one occasion, I might add. Everyone who knows and loves me has their theory about why I've preferred to be a young man's fool.

Theory #1: Being an Alpha female, I like to be in control

Theory #2: Being a therapist, I thrive on a good project

The theory I like most comes from a good friend

Theory #3: She says she thinks I love younger men because of my spritely, youthful personality, and most men who are older simply can't keep up.

I want to go with door #3. But the one that resonates most truthfully for me is the one that, when I heard it for the first time, hit like a gong at the core of my belly. This one came from a spiritual mentor and dear friend, and I quote:

Theory #4: *"I think that one of your cosmic assignments in this lifetime Tamyra, is to raise good boys to great men. You do a damn good job, you know."*

CHAPTER 5
RAISING BOYS TO GOOD MEN

After hearing my friend say those words, I thought of all the women I knew to which "raising good boys to great men" could apply. I recalled a pivotal conversation with one of my dearest friends. And though that conversation was shared a long time ago, it left an indelible mark. It went something like this:

Frankly, and without a stitch of modesty, I do a damn good job raising boys into men. My first proof of this came one day when I drove up to my first husband's home to collect our four children, and noticed a staggeringly large bouquet of flowers sitting on the table near the bay window. Looking at that arrangement, I was overwhelmed with painful memories, and as I backed out of the driveway, kids safely transported to their other home, I realized I had taught him to do this. I had begged this same man for years for a bouquet of "nothing says I love you like...roses." I begged to eventual hopelessness, until quite tragically, with one-and-one-half feet out the door, emotional baggage packed and ready to go, the flowers began to thunder in.

I remember the evening the last arrangement came walking through the door in the hands of my pale and worn out husband. I remember what I said that night as

I wept out loud: "Why couldn't you have given me flowers when I needed them? I think you're only giving them to me now because you're the one in need."

Heart wrenching to hear and easy to relate. We women always know this truth. It's why we often say with heavy-hearted despair to our friends and therapists: "It was too little too late." We say those words because we suspect that in the end, they were still taking care of themselves. We suspect they heard our final cries and bought the flowers or the trip to Milan so that their own lives might not be interrupted, and even then, we fear, we know, deep in our sad and worn out hearts, they still didn't do it for us.

I suspect that through her pain, my friend taught her first husband, as I did, to give his second wife flowers as marital insurance – a preemptive strike against the painful withering of love that is lost through neglect. I also hope that she and I taught our men folk to give their new wives flowers because she is beautiful, because she is utterly worthy of receiving them. I hope we taught them to give flowers simply because that is what a grown man possessing grown up love does. And I hope perhaps that my next man has been taught that as well.

CHAPTER 6
STAIRWAY TO HEAVEN

With Ryan, I believe my greatest gift to his manhood was my consistent demonstration of my own faith. I met him when he was in his early twenties and mildly agnostic. But I strongly believe that by my regularly attending church, partaking in many other forms of spiritual and emotional growth work, and inviting him along, I had a part in his more fully embracing a power greater than his human self. In connecting him to some of the most conscious people I knew, I witnessed him develop more and more connection with his own divine nature, and branch further out into his own spiritual connections with others.

In the last year of our relationship, I began to feel that our new spiritual bond was inspiring a deeper and more loving connection between us. How could it not? I thought. We now have a spiritual context to trust the path of our relationship's unfolding. Ironically — or is it "paradoxically"? — even as our relationship continued to be on-again, off-again throughout 2008, we began to attend church regularly as a family. Ryan and I also began doing charity work together with a prison ministry in the spring of 2009, and for the first time in 18 months, I began to have real hope. Come early July 2009, however, shortly after a fantastic trip to Florida for the fourth of July, and in the middle of preparing and training for our trip to Angola Prison together, our relationship took a quantum leap into the dark depths of relationship hell.

Though the details will remain forever between the two of us and a few trusted friends, there was an incident that prompted the blunt ending. At the same time, I do appreciate that we both manifested that blunt ending through years of difficulty alternating between trying to adapt, trying to control and trying to surrender. I believe we manifested all of it, every last minute of it for our collective spiritual growth. The kind of limb stretching growth that on my disconnected days I refer to as heart wrenching; growth that on my spiritually connected days I refer to as expanding. And frankly it was both heart wrenching and expanding at the same time.

I already know this pain I feel today will eventually give way to my blessing him and the woman he's connected with now on their journey forward. But honestly, I don't have it in me to bless them just yet. It's been only six months since our final descent, and six months is not nearly long enough for me to mend that heartbreak. And though I know it's for the greatest good of all concerned, and clearly for my own good that I bless them, I'm simply not ready. My heart needs more mending. Perhaps it needs, I need, more reassurance that this dividing of our son's life into two households, this shortening by half of his time with both of us, is truly for the best.

I adore my son Gabriel and cherish my time with him so completely that it's painful to come home after work and not have him here. He's only 8, and there's still so much of his young life left to be lived, so much precious time that I'm going to be cheated out of - Ice-cream on the way home from school, coco and board games before bedtime, stories told in the remains of the day, and snuggling with a good movie, a bowl of popcorn and a warm blanket. All cut in half by Ryan's and my inability to truly understand what it would take to make our relationship kinder, gentler and manageable together.

I want to be mad at someone, but there is no one,

not even God, the Devil, Ryan or myself on which to wield this anger. There is not one tangible person, place or thing at which to point a finger for this tragedy. It's just the misfortune of life itself that does the robbing. And the only upside to this that I can see is that I cherish my precious son and my precious time with him exponentially more so now. I've stopped taken any time with him for granted.

And despite a good argument for "Where was God when...?" six months later I reach down a little deeper and I feel that my faith is still solid. It is solid, because I don't just believe: I already know that Spirit never sends a landslide through one path without diverting my steps toward a more magnificent vista. My life has proven this over, and over, and over again. I know Spring will always follow Winter, simply because I have not one shred of evidence to the contrary. I know this cold, cold Winter will be succeeded by another radiant bloom of Spring. I can already feel the energy of this Spring experience warming and mending my tattered spirit—mending it deep into the subatomic particles that lie below the deepest muscles of my heart.

And if by chance we do earn points with the

Universe for helping to herd its sheep, then I might have moved a rung up that stairway to Heaven by bringing Ryan part way home. Honestly though, I don't suspect that's the case, (the earning rungs up the golden ladder part that is,) and I doubt there is any reward greater than the joy I feel in knowing my second son's father deeply believes in a power higher than the human ego. Perhaps it's my own ego speaking here.

CHAPTER 7
LADY GODIVA BARING IT IN THE COLD

JANUARY 10, 2010

It's a Sunday night in January. No roses and no husband to come home to. It feels ridiculously, unseasonably cold. It's below freezing, and I'm feeling chilled to the bone tonight. I just left the warmth of my former spouse's home. I left my son sleeping soundly there after cuddling close and reading a chapter of his favorite book series. I left after making some joint preparations for his first day of his new school tomorrow.

Truthfully, I had to tear myself away—I had to tear myself away from my beautiful, warm, sleeping son, and a scene that someone looking in from the cold might mistake for sweet family harmony: a sleeping son, and two parents sitting at the table making preparations for the new week.

I had to tear myself away late on a Sunday evening from their warm and cozy home, and return to my own, mine and my son's in the half-time when he's not with his father. Most nights are not this difficult, but tonight as I turn the key and open the door to solitude, my home feels particularly chilly. Some from the temperature (I had it down to 60 degrees,) but more chill in my bones from the reminder tonight that my beloved son and beloved former spouse are together on this cold night, and I am in my cold, dark home alone—not with myself...but alone.

I decide to console myself, and reach for comfort in the same way any sensible woman might. I reach for the box of Godiva Chocolates Ryan gave me for Christmas. I choose carefully. If I'm going to consume an extra 100 calories before bedtime, it is going to be a worthy pursuit.

I chose a truffle with a dark chocolate center. I take a bite, and before I can savor the delicate, impeccable taste of this little ball of nirvana, I remember that this is the same sized box that he used to give my daughter for Christmas. I use to get the large box. Mid bite, I realize "she," his new love, got the large box for Christmas. I've been downsized. I gulp hard with this latest reminder – I'm no longer at the gooey center of his life.

And in that mid-bite I felt a twinge of shame – the kind of shame that comes with feeling greedy.

After all, this is a "high-class problem," as a friend would say. We are talking about a very high-end box of chocolates – even if it was the medium size...so, I take another bite. The chocolate, my favorite chocolate, lands bitter sweet on my tongue. There is only one thing left when chocolate fails to comfort: I write.

CHAPTER 8
BUYING A NEW CAR ALL BY MYSELF

Still mid-January, I stumble upon AFLO (Another F-in' Learning Opportunity.) Like a boil coming to a head, this particular AFLO fleshes out my fears about doing things alone that I've long considered "men's work." One of the hardest things about being a single woman in the middle of my life is that ever-present ghost of men past. You know, the ghost that shows up to haunt and torment when the faucet starts to leak, or the cabinet door comes off the hinge — haunts and torments with a reminder that I am alone, and because I have not been alone before, I have never acquired the skills to be handy around the house...and truthfully, I don't want to learn to be handy around the house. I still want a handy dandy man to do the faucet-fixing and the re-hinging of the cabinet doors, as well as be an exceptional lover, provider and all-around good guy.

Such was the case when my car died a sudden death in early January. Yes, as is always the case, the car I had just finished paying off several months prior, and was hoping to drive a couple more years before surrendering to another note, began to have a multitude of problems that made it impossible to keep. One major expense after another forced me for the first time into the testosterone-fueled world of car sales and car salesmen.

But despite my high anxiety about purchasing a vehicle, I was determined to purchase one all by myself. I mean, "with myself." And, you know what? I did it. I did it, and if I do say so myself, I used such an exquisite combination of male and female energy on this purchase, that I know Carl Jung (who introduced the concept of the integration of yin and yang to the West) would have been proud.

It was both exhilarating and remotely terrifying at the same time. Sitting across from a well-seasoned salesman – another strikingly tall, dark and handsome, well-dressed man, I felt scared, but resolved to get what I needed – no more, and no less.

At one point in the negotiations, I looked across at him, right into his determined but kind eyes, and thought, *You know, we're both here to get what we need.* In that moment I felt both deep compassion for him and for myself. Having just talked with another salesman, I learned that sales had been down at the dealership by forty-two percent. That meant that the man sitting across from me, a man who drives a luxury vehicle to complement his high-end suit, must be, to say the least, a little tense himself these days. Sitting across from him, and being a friend of a friend of his, I know we both have a budget to meet, kids in college and a lifestyle that we cherish.

There was, however, one point in the deal when I almost gave up and walked away – not as a smoke-screen-and-mirror ploy, but just in sheer exhaustion. After almost two hours into the car-buying process, we were still $100 off from what I wanted to pay per month – what I could reasonably pay per month. But instead of leaving, I paused from almost opting to take the flight end of the flight-or-fight response, and said a prayer that went something like this: *Dear Spirit, this man and I both have needs to meet – needs that I'm sure are much the same. Please help us both walk away from this deal feeling taken care of.*

It was only a matter of minutes before he found my same vehicle, in the same color, but a less acces-sorized version for a few thousand less. (Most people call those fancy things that jack up the price "options," but they look like accessories to me, in much the same way my Our Lady of Guadalupe earrings dangling from my ears accessorized an already fully-equipped me today.)

Despite the fact that I knew this seasoned salesman would have preferred to sell me the "limited" version of my already expensive vehicle, I stayed centered in what I needed and kept stating: "These things are nice, but I am really not the kind of woman who needs them. What I need is reliability, safety and an affordable car note each month. Could you please see if you have this same vehicle for less?" And he did, and I purchased.

In the end, I drove away happy – though I must admit that CD player access from the steering wheel and the seat that warmed my bottom on this uncharacteristic 20 degree southern Louisiana day would make nice accessories for someone who could truly afford the "luxury" of them. In the same end, I think my very professional salesman was happy too, in part because I was not a difficult client. He, in turn, was not a difficult salesman. He was the kind of man I will refer whenever I'm asked who I might recommend.

So...what I learned today from negotiating my very first unaccompanied car deal, is that I can do a difficult "Alpha" thing, like negotiating a car sale without an Alpha male to negotiate for me. If the truth be known, I did have my dear friend Vince lined up as my "lifeline" had I needed him. I asked, and he eagerly agreed, but in the end, I felt the confidence to go it alone. My clients report a similar experience when they have a script of Xanax. They tell me that they rarely need to use it, but just knowing it's there if they find themselves in a panic helps to keep the panic away. Such was the case, I suspect, with my friend and lifeline Vince.

I'll graciously admit that despite the fact that I was unaccompanied at the dealership, there were lots of people behind the scene. It took a village to buy this car – my Village – the one I've built, the one that I refer to as my support team, my Sangha. Knowing Vince had my back, having my best girl friend who just purchased a car herself give me a "you can do it!" pep talk, and Facebook querying friends for dealerships and good salesmen helped me walk in confidently, and leave feeling strong and capable. As the saying goes, "It takes a village to raise a child,"

and it also takes a village to survive mid-life singlehood with grace and good-humor.

CHAPTER 9
A TANTRIC GOD APPEARS

Still savoring the chemically hypnotic new car smells, I find myself well into the first week of February: one week before our beloved Saints won the most Super of all Super Bowls, and two weeks before the fusion of Valentine's day and Mardi Gras weekend here in southern Louisiana. This week, the Universe gifted me with a visit from a Tantric mentor of mine: a man that is sharpened to the likes of a Greek God; a man who reminds me of the statue David. The Universe graced me this cold week of February with a learning so magnificent, that it allowed for the release of long-standing resentment of the relationship too beautiful to leave and too difficult in which to stay. It left me with a deeper acceptance for what is, and it left me with a desire to wish goodness to come to my former spouse and his current girlfriend.

I want to state here that this tantric god of a man and mentor is blissfully married to a tantric goddess of a woman. He's not from the Middle East, but from Chile. Like many South American men, he is of

Northern European descent, both in stature and in chiseled good looks. The following story reveals the gift of this man's illuminating presence, the healing power of his hands, and the transcendent properties of the words he spoke that are with me still today.

This gift of a man, and this gift of further illumination, started, as is always the case for me, with a strong intention. My intention for the early part of this year, shortly after writing Chapter 6, was to release any standing resentment, as well as any longing in my heart, for Ryan. And along with releasing standing resentment, I also wanted to be able to wish him a long and happy life without me.

As best as I can gather, I was able to manifest my intention this week through two healing modalities, and a furthering conversation with Vince, the same friend who was willing to accompany me with my car purchase. I'll get to the conversation with my friend later, but for now, back to the experience with my tantric God.

The first was the actual psychic/energetic healing that took place in our bodywork together. An expert at both Thai Massage and Tantric energy work, he massaged and manipulated my body and my soul into a state of grace. With his strong muscles and intuitive sixth-sense, he massaged the demons of victimhood and jealousy right out of my lower three chakras (where at least three other of the seven deadly sins reside as well).

A clear defining moment came mid-way into our session when my mentor mounted the massage table and straddled my hips, all 6'3" inches of the man, and lifted my upper back off the table. Completely trusting and relaxed for the first half of the session, I began to shift into a tenser, tighter space – a sense of clear and present danger arose.

After cupping my shoulder blades tenderly in his hands, and drawing me closer toward him, he slid his hands a little further down below the back of my ribcage. As he continued to guide me gently closer to himself, opening both the front of my rib cage and my heart chakra with subtle graceful movement, he noticed that my body begun to stiffen against his embrace. I felt the flooding of visceral fear course through my veins and strike a harsh, cold chord right into the middle of my heart – right into the middle of this exquisite moment. As I tightened further, I began to sense that he felt every subtle movement in my muscles. He did, and he asked:

"What is going on inside of you Tamyra?"

As soon as he asked the question, I felt the answer well up deep from inside of me, but the words stayed lodged in my throat. My body, however, told everything. I involuntary leaned toward him, white knuckles gripping his thickened biceps with the same hands that moments ago were opened and relaxed, and as I did, the sheet feel down my front side and landed across my hips. But in the end, having my flesh exposed wasn't nearly as unnerving in that moment as having my soul exposed with the question that was asked once more.

"What is going on inside of you?"

Hearing those words I began to shake. Clinging to his arms more tightly, I finally managed through a choking of tears to dislodge the words and whisper:

"I'm afraid...I'm afraid you'll drop me, and I'll fall."

In the next moment, still straddling me, still holding the back of my ribs in his strong, sensitive hands, he asked me to open my eyes and look at him. I opened them. Looking into my eyes, and my eyes now looking into his, he said in a commanding but tender voice:

"Tamyra, I will NOT drop you. I will not let you go. And I will NOT let you fall."

Amazingly, I believed him. And it wasn't because he had a strong grip on my shoulders – he had the strength to hold me up with the tip of one pinky – I believed he would not drop me because I "felt" the truth coming from inside of him, to the inside of me.

So in that moment of truth, I exhaled, I let go, and let my upper back yield, and my chest unfold like a blooming lotus. I let myself open and expand into his big, strong arms, and the tears came tumbling down. In the next moment, with my aching heart chakra opened even wider, totally unsuspecting of what would come next, he placed his lips on the warm, shaking flesh above my heart. First I heard then felt him begin to chant a Tibetan prayer right into that soft, pliable heart space.

He could have been chanting for hours or for only moments, I lost all concept of time. These moments in life are not constructed with earth time. Rather they're made of stardust that lingers from and for eternity. However long it took, it was one of the most sensual (not sexual) moments of my life. He was chanting, right into my beating heart. I felt a cracking of my heart space. I felt it crack wide open and something deeply lodged came energetically oozing out. After a mystical moment in time and more tears – this time healing tears – breathlessly I managed to eke out the words:

"Ahh...that stuff was old."

I left the table minutes later feeling more fully alive than I could recall. I also left with a deep knowing that there are men who have the capability to hold a woman tenderly but firmly in the palms of their hands without dropping her.

My tantric mentor told me at the end of our session that I had to stop dating men under forty. I needed a man who could handle me in a direct but tender way. I needed, according to him, one with both authority and understanding. And he also said; "Tamyra, men aren't worth much to women before the age of forty anyway." He is forty-six.

On a literal, emotional level, the body work was

symbolic of the release of mistrust in men. I realized in that moment I had never been in a serious relationship with a man over thirty nine. In order to trust myself with another man, I needed one who has truly come into his own. A man who had the maturity to hold my heart tenderly in the palm of his hands, and at the same time be fearless in his pursuit of happiness. I needed a mature, well-integrated man, because I, along the way am becoming a mature and well-integrated woman.

CHAPTER 10
YIN AND YANG

FEBRUARY 4, 2010

The second part of the healing took place with this same mentor, in a much less dramatic but equally poignant way. It started as a simple dialogue among friends and culminated in a heightened awareness of how much I needed a partner whose masculine and feminine energies danced together like Shiva and Shakti. At the end of my five day visit with my mentor, I was inspired with a new belief that men with qualities such as his are uncommon, but do exist, and that men like that are well worth waiting for.

On this fateful week, and as other interactions with my mentor took place, I began to experience a deeper understanding of how the two great relationships of my life unraveled. They unraveled from our mutual lack of understanding of how to dance with someone whose energies are equal to but different from our own. As a result, I could not fully trust either of my former partners to keep me from falling. In other words, the difficulty of the dance made it impossible for me to ever feel fully understood. I want to be clear here: these weren't their shortcomings any more than they were my own.

My first husband was physically strong, a hearty Alpha from good Dutch peasant stock. And I came from a long line of virile males and females from hearty Cajun and Italian stock. I understood him on a deeply primordial level. Like our parents and their parents before them, we were self-made business men and women who knew how to single-mindedly forge a path to success.

My first husband's directness and strong character are still attractive to me, but I believe our undoing was our inability to connect emotionally. He was Spock to my McCoy. So when I needed to talk about deeper matters of the heart, or needed a strong warm shoulder to cry on, I got a logical explanation as to why I shouldn't feel the way I felt. The same reasonable and logical explanations many women friends and clients tell me they get from their beloved partners. Like these women folk, much of the time I felt alone and left to heal my past and present emotional wounds on my own. There was no net of emotional support to fall into when I teetered too close to the edge.

In contrast, Ryan was sensitive and intuitive – a strong Beta with good Alpha qualities. He was tender, highly emotional (this worked in my favor as often as it did not), and he could listen to me when I needed someone to listen. But at times when I couldn't do it alone, I often felt desperate for ground that wasn't constantly moving under my feet.

So with more clarity about how difficult the fits between my two long time partners and I were, I began to notice the rapid releasing of long held as well as more recent resentments. My work with my tantric mentor has me awakening more deeply to the opinion that both my first and my second spouse could not give me more, nor did they give me less than they had to give me. And even if they didn't clearly recognize my needs, (in part because I didn't clearly recognize my own,) I know now they still tried their best to take care of me.

I hear my inner critic right now, a scolding, punitive voice within that I refer to as Miss Savoie (Pronounced Sov wa' in French, and I will get to an explanation of her later) saying, *"You're never satisfied, Tamyra Faith."* Perhaps not Miss Savoie, but I'm much clearer today about what does and does not satisfy me. What does and does nourish and sustain me – much clearer.

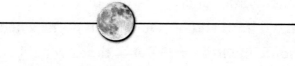

CHAPTER 11
ENLIGHTENED MOMENTS

Throughout the whole next week, more insight came flooding in. Flashbacks of heart-ripping conversations came to center stage. As I held each of these emotional tsunamis in the context of my new learnings, the heart-wrenching disconnections began for the first time, to make sense. As Dave Mason's song suggests: *There ain't no good guy / there ain't no bad guy / there's only you and me and we just disagree.* With respect to Ryan and me, I needed him to be more decisive about what he needed and desired from me and from life. He needed me to be more yielding to the time it took for him to know these things himself. Tragically, in our inability to give what was needed to the other, in our inability to truly understand the dynamic between us, we unconsciously, unintentionally tore at each other's spirits as we continuously tried to make the other more like the self.

The third and final insight in this series came later that week in a conversation with my dear friend Vince. I was telling Vince the story of my tantric body work experience and how much resentment I'd released. I told Vince there was just one part left, and that despite my deep desire to do so, I couldn't seem to manifest. It was the part where I truly, deeply and sincerely wished Ryan and his new love a happy life together.

Vince, listening contemplatively and intensely as he always does, asked me why I thought this might be so. I thought about this for a few moments, then said:

"If he's happy now with the new woman, and remains so, he would continue to believe the demise of our relationship was all my fault."

Again listening very intensely, he asked; "Well could you wish ENLIGHTENMENT for him instead?"

Enlightenment? EUREKA! What a beautiful idea. I saw the absolute divinity in that question. If I wished for him enlightenment then enlightenment might give him the insight to realize his own part in our unhinging. His enlightenment would eventually lead to his happiness, but he would also begin to know how deeply I hurt from his unskilled words and actions. And as my sage of a daughter reminded me recently while on a sunset stroll, "What we wish for others, Mom, comes back to us tenfold."

I had been wishing great difficulties for Ryan in his new partnership — not because I wanted either of them unhappy, but because I wanted the Universe to show him his part in our failing. Not so amazingly, I was getting similar lessons in return. Ah, karma, baby...but I like this notion of blessing him with enlightenment. By wishing him enlightenment, I just might become a little more enlightened in return...and who couldn't use a little more enlightenment on any given day?

That night I expressed my gratitude to Vince for his wisdom. Today, I wish Ryan enlightenment, and may enlightenment lead us both to deeper happiness as well as deeper understanding.

CHAPTER 12
SOULMATE SECRET AND THE LIST

Amazing how this works. With a little bit of effort and a very strong intention, I, with the support of great friends, have freed myself from the oppression of resentment, cleaned and cleared my heart's closet and prepared room for great new things to come.

My beautiful daughter recently gave me her copy of a book she read shortly before meeting her phenomenal boyfriend Cody. It's called The Soulmate Secret. It's a book about preparing yourself, readying yourself to find your true love and soul mate. I remember the night some months ago when Claire shared with me that Cody had every quality on the list that the author, Arielle Ford, recommend she write. But she added, and I paraphrase; "Mom, the amazing thing is that God was gracious enough to add a few more qualities that I didn't even know to ask for." Wow...

Right now the book is an affirmation of what I'm already doing – a navigational guide or compass, so to speak, affirming that I'm on the right track. Much of what I've already accomplished above is suggested in the beginning part of the book – clearing emotional space to make room for "bigger love."

I already started my list. So once again, *The Soulmate Secret* is affirming my way. My list has actually been more like a living document that I keep adding to over time. Over the last two years, I've been compiling bits and pieces of it as a way of speaking into the depravation I've felt for my entire life. But I think I'm now ready to add to my list from a more positive place – a place of joyful anticipation of abundant love.

My list is written in a red-velvet journal with a red rhinestone heart as its centerpiece. I didn't set out for this journal to be all about love, but perhaps that particular red-velvet studded heart journal called to me for just that purpose. My daughter and I have a New Year's Eve ritual of going together to the bookstore to purchase our new journals for the upcoming year. We have a lot of fun doing it. We help each other choose, and this, with her agreement, was the journal I chose for the year 2009 – the year Ryan left for good.

So I've been compiling my list for over a year now.

It started as a plea to the Universe to quench the thirst of my barren heart, but today I'm intent on adding, yes, adding from a space of abundance rather than of lack.

The first list was a bulleted itemized list I wrote on the front inside cover of the journal. It reads like this:

- Emotionally healthy
- Self-insightful
- Gentle with my wounded parts
- Always kind, never mean-spirited or insulting
- Inspiring, enthusiastic and enrolling
- Plans and initiates great adventures
- Keeps a yard, and a garage, too
- Can afford a beautiful home
- Strong work ethic
- His default button is happy (like when I call him during the day he sounds happy to hear from me and is very happy to see me when I come home.)
- Asks me: "How can I help to make your life better?"
- Accepting of feedback. Not quick to defend. Listens to my concerns and hurts.
- Compassionate when I have bad moods and doesn't need to shift them by shaming me or going away. Might even ask what he can do to help.
- Slow to anger – in other words: patient
- More mature than anyone I've been with yet

And then toward the middle of the journal, in a multitude of brightly colored Sharpies (it doesn't escape me right now that a Sharpie is a kind of permanent marker), I found another list, less in bullet form and more as a running narrative:

He is honest and has great integrity. He is a professional and is well-established in his career. He is ambitious, industrious in his career and loves what he does. He is alpha, virile, athletic, poised, and strong. He is beautiful inside and out. He is masculine, and I am deeply aroused by him physically. Full head of hair and taller than 5' 8". He is intelligent, decisive, exuberant, adventurous, spontaneous, extremely confident, has boundless energy, and "clean" power. There is a playful lightness about him, and people are drawn to him. He enjoys my poetry and literature.

He looks at me adoringly, gazes across the room and lets me know with that look that I am magnificent and deeply loved and lovable. He has great balance in his life in work and play. We mentor each other and together create financial freedom so that we can both work and play as much as we want to. He is a loving, attentive father and spends quality time with the people he loves. He is generous and giving, and charitable with his resources and his time. He always believes he has more than enough to share.

He is physically healthy. He exercises and eats well. He is single and heterosexual, and did I already mention available?

Woe... That's one tall order, and I'm not even finished yet.

CHAPTER 13
PLAY DATES WITH MYSELF

It's been several weeks since my tantric adventure, yet I'm still humming and vibrating with the openness and freedom of emotional release.

I'm noticing on this penultimate day in February that it's been years since I've experienced this level of peace and equanimity. More honestly, it may have been since my twenty-three year old son and twenty-two year old daughter were in early grade school that I felt this self-connected. I was so enamored with the delights of being a doting stay-at-home mother of precious younglings back then, that I never noticed what was missing.

I'm remembering now that the first strong yearnings for a companion who could dive with me to the emotional depths I was needing to get to surfaced back when my daughter entered kindergarten and my son was in first grade. My first real feelings of loneliness and emptiness arrived while still tucked safely inside the womb of an outwardly-thriving relationship.

Little did I know back then that the stirrings were not just a longing for a deeper connection with my mate, but were also a longing for a deeper connection with myself. Over and over again in my 20 years as a psychotherapist, I see this happening to women in their mid-thirties: this wake-up call to themselves. And it often starts with a thought similar to this one:

"I've been taking care of everyone else's needs for so long now, that I have no idea who I am or what my own needs are. I'm also looking around and wondering who's taking care of me besides me?"

I've learned over time that if this longing is not tended to, great difficulty is imminent. So, fifteen years after having these same thoughts and asking these same questions of myself, I realize this current quest for balance in my life is a result of cosmic stirrings that began fifteen years earlier. These divine portals to quality time and quality care of myself truly began to reveal themselves the day my youngest went to school.

Now smack dab in mid-life, some would call this a crisis. Some would think these were symptoms of empty-nest. I however, call this awareness a miracle.

And who would have guessed that finding balance between my needs and others would take me to the point of truly enjoying spending long periods of time alone getting to know myself? Yes, time alone, not by myself, but more appropriately, with myself. These are deliciously happy times getting to know myself and my needs and preferences. And I've noticed the quest for self-understanding is made easier without the outside influence of a spouse's own preferences on my energy and on my time.

Now take into consideration, please, that what I call long periods of time is a relative term. I'm a true extrovert (one who recharges my emotional battery by being in the company of others), so "being alone for long periods of time" means an evening alone or a day to myself. Unless it's a trip to write, I'm not the kind of person who relishes the thought of taking a solo flight to a foreign land, or even a long weekend alone at the beach. Though admittedly, I've had limited but pleasurable exposure to both solo transatlantic flights and days on the beach, so who knows what will come of this romantic relationship I'm developing with myself? For now, an evening or a day alone is a stretch for a woman who can counsel clients all day, then get in my car on the way home and call family and friends to catch up.

Introverts sometimes want to tell us extroverts that "we're afraid to be alone" – just as we want to tell our introverted counterparts that "they're afraid to be with people." But as I grow and mature in my understanding of temperament and personality, I believe the role our neurological hardwiring plays in determining how much joy or woe we experience in relationship to others cannot be ignored.

So for me enjoying an evening alone with myself, or a day of yoga, or browsing the farmer's market is quite fulfilling. And as my life and time as a single women of mid-age progresses, I find myself (rather than by default) intentionally choosing to make play dates with myself – play dates to do whatever it is that comes up for me in the moment-to-moment pleasure of my own company.

And though I can't yet connect the dots perfectly, I believe that unshackeling and exorcising the ghosts of relationships past cleared a significant space for me to pursue a deeper relationship with myself.

CHAPTER 14

I AM READYING MYSELF FOR YOU

And with all that said above, I also have a visceral, intuitive, full-body knowing that the unshackeling and freeing of all that emotional pain is not only connecting me more to myself, but is also beckoning my strong, handsome, sensual man as well. It's truly a knowing. I don't know when. I don't know how. I don't know where. But what I do know is that he is already looking for me, talking to me in his dreams. I can feel him. He's palpable.

I know I won't have to go looking for him, cruise the dance halls, churches and sports fields for him. He will just appear, in all his glory, right before me at an unsuspecting moment, and in that very same instant, I'll know it's him. True to form for an Alpha, he'll show-straight shooting, obvious interest in me. No games. Yes, absolutely no games. I just know this. As I've written in my journal, "I don't know how, when or where, but it has been determined. It has been written, and he will arrive in more splendor and glory than I have even imagined."

I think the knowing started one night when I was

sitting out on my patio. It was a recent starlit, unseasonably cold night. Sitting quietly, I heard the voice of God. I've heard the voice of God now on several occasions: once when I was sitting on my living room floor, begging for forgiveness for breaking one of the Ten Commandments – a big one. I heard a clear and present command say inside my head, *I forgave you a long time ago, now it's time to forgive yourself.* And in that very next moment, I did.

I heard God's voice another time on a ski trip to Colorado. It happened late one afternoon. As is my ritual, at the end of the day, I head to the chair right before it closes, and tell the attendant I want the last chair up. Then when I get to the top I patiently wait for all the rest of the skiers to ski down, and then I descend the mountain alone. On that particular day, perched atop the trail head, waiting for all the other skiers to ski down the slope, overlooking the virgin white valley, in awe of my surroundings, in awe of my love for skiing, I gleefully say out loud, "God, what a great invention. Too bad you don't ski." And to my utter amazement, I heard him just as clearly reply, *What do you mean I don't ski? I ski because I'M YOU! I'm God expressed as you. I experience your passion, through you – especially when you are in this place of gratitude.*

This time the voice of God spoke in that same commanding mountain top way, that way that leaves no doubt that the words came not from me, but through me, as God said, *"This will be the last cold winter you ever spend."* And in that moment my body rumbled with the sound of that voice, and I knew deep in my heartache he was telling me that with or without a partner, I would be okay. Frankly, I'd prefer to have a partner, so with that in mind, I've taken to the patio on several cold evenings since hearing that command, and with coffee or tea in hand, I sit and talk to my beloved, and it sounds something like this:

Hello Love. I feel you thinking about me. Wondering where I am. Well, I'm here. I'm readying myself for you. I'm getting to know myself so deeply that when you meet me, you'll know who I am instantly, because I'll know who I am. And I will know who you are. I feel you coming to me now. I feel you preparing and readying yourself for me. Hi my love. Hi, I am so excited to meet you.

And it may be five minutes or five months or five years. It doesn't really matter to me, because I KNOW you'll be well worth waiting for and that I'll be okay in the meantime. Yes, in the meantime, I'm having the time of my life falling more deeply in love with myself and with life on life's terms...yes, I am preparing myself for you... In God's good time.

Truthfully, the nights have been physically colder than normal here in the deep South. It's snowed twice this year. It usually snows once every five years. But my heart's been warm with love for myself, for my life, and for all that's good in my life. I'm warm with an unshakable trust that all is in Divine order, including, but not limited to, the coming of my beloved.

And to secure the deal, I've called upon my beloved mentor, Andy Shurr, now working from the other side, to assist in our journey toward each other. Andy, who transcended this earth two years ago, was the kind of man who didn't just talk (though he loved to do that), but he walked his talk – not on occasion, but with each step he took. Andy was one of the most conscious and awakened spirits I've ever known. I learned much about how to be a good person and better counselor from him. And Andy believed in true love. Andy believed in Soul Mates. Andy found his Soul Mate, Joy, in the middle of his own life and was married to her for the remainder of it, living a long, happy and healthy life into his 80's. So with my dear friend Andy to illuminate the way, I do whole heartedly believe I can do the same.

Thank God I believe that kind of love is attainable thanks to Andy and Joy, and other wonderful couple mentors, like my friends Peggy and Nolan, and Charlie and Linda Bloom. With these loving couples' assistance, and with God's promise to give me the Kingdom, I'm readying myself to give and receive that kind of love. That is, I'm readying myself for him by giving that kind of love to myself today.

Andy, I know you were with me that night on the patio.

CHAPTER 15
THE PLEASURE OF THEIR COMPANY

"Mom, where are you?"

*"Matt, I'm at the park with your brother.
Where are you?"*

*"I'm on my way home from diving Port Fourchon.
I'll be home in an hour."*

*"Oh, wow, I didn't know you were in this part of
the world. I'll be home soon Son.
Can you stay for dinner?"*

*"I'm staying the night.
Heading back to school tomorrow."*

"Wonderful...I'll see you in a few then."

Of course I'm coming straight home. I'm dropping everything I've planned for the rest of the afternoon and evening to come home to spend a precious few moments with my twenty-three year old son: a young man who has life gripped tightly by the testicles; a young man whose life experience has taught him that the earth, moon and stars revolve around nothing greater than offering him pleasure; a young man who has granted his mother a precious few moments of his exhilarating, overflowing life before going back to finish his final semester in Chemical Engineering.

We leave the park earlier than planned. When I get home he's soundly and sweetly asleep on the couch. His favorite channel, National Geographic Adventure, is blaring in the background. Frankly, his life is a National Geographic Adventure. He's as at home on the top of the Grand Tetons hunting elk and looking for grizzlies as he is 100 feet below the Gulf of Mexico spear fishing red snapper and amberjack. I feel terribly proud and terribly frightened. He is a fearless Alpha with wanderlust, intellect, and a deeply soulful yearning to understand God on God's terms, rather than man's. That wanderlust soul of his takes him to places I'd dare not tread.

He's always been adventurous, and he's always been equally soulful and contemplative. Once, at about the age of six, he asked me if I thought Adam and Eve had belly buttons. Then, another time in his teens, I asked him how he and his beautiful young girlfriend where doing. He frowned, and said "Mom, she's beautiful and fun and loving but she doesn't look at the stars the same way that I do." I fell silent, and I swallowed hard, because I got it. I got it because I knew that place from which my eldest was speaking. He was already yearning for a soul mate – a lover to share that ineffable quality of connection that occurs when two spirits look up and see the wonders of Universe in the same way. I knew in that moment that he would never be able to settle for less. Ahh, he's got the curse of wanderlust – the inability to settle, and I think he got it from his mother's pirate blood.

We get to dinner later that night. I've invited his younger sister by 17 months and her boyfriend to join us. Claire and Cody look like Barbie and Ken. A gorgeous Aryan, All-American Couple – like Matthew, both athletes with academic scholarships to college. All three of these young people are well-integrated within their confident bodies. Cody is a basketball player/poet with a wit as sharp as a butcher's knife. Claire, graduating college a year early, is a cross country state champion, chomping at the bit to finish social work school and work with the aging. She and Cody look at the stars in the same wondrous way that Matt and his gorgeous, graceful and gifted fiancée Michelle and I do. There's always a synergy in the room when we're all together, and it's palpable tonight.

Sitting at the table with these three beautiful young people teaming with exuberance and joie de vivre, I have a deep appreciation for what incredibly charming, intelligent dinner companions I'm graced with this evening. In that same moment, I also get how blessed I am to have adult children that I consider wonderful dinner companions. And I get in that moment, how blessed I am that they turned out alright! Thank God, they turned out alright.

Shortly into dinner, the ever rivalrous siblings get to doing their thing. Claire begins to share that Scientologists believe in eating placenta. She announces that there's even a placenta pizza. We all throw her a look of suspicion at the same time. Of course, her brother challenges her. He whips out his iPhone from his pocket and makes a quick (and I daresay novel) search for placenta pizza.

In moments his eyes get big and wide, and he throws his head back with hearty laughter. There is indeed a Placenta Pizza, he announces. It's a place to eat pizza in Placenta – Placenta, California. We all roar with laughter. Then he informs us that there's a Placenta Delivery Service... this time, begging the attention of people sitting near us with even louder laughter. I have tears in my eyes at this point, and I'm laughing so hard I have to slap something. I slap my thighs and stomp my feet over and over as we continue to laugh at the offerings in Placenta.

Finally he announces that there's a Placenta Boys' and Girls' club. At this point we're all laughing so hysterically that I see from the corner of my eye that the people around us are just a little interrupted by it all. But I don't care. To laugh often and laugh loud with my offspring and friends is much of what my gloriously simple life is about. Again, I catch a wave of gratitude. I'm grateful for this cherished time. I am grateful that they turned out alright.

As a younger professional, I wrote a book that is still in print: *How to Raise Happy, Loving, Emotionally Intelligent Kids.* I've often been struck as an older adult how lofty a title that was considering my children were half grown at the time I wrote it.

I reflect a little more tonight. Was it lofty? Or did I just intuitively know that no matter what I did, the hard wiring of temperament and my deep adoration for them would eventually play a much larger role than my parenting skills ever could? Or perhaps the title of the book was more like an intention spoken out loud. Yes, I intended to raise Happy, Loving, Emotionally Intelligent Kids. And perhaps too, despite my many shortcomings, because I spoke it out loud in that way, the Universe obliged me with three wonderful children and with a very insightful book.

Outside, it's another unseasonably blustery night in southern Louisiana, but it's wonderfully warm inside. It's toasty warm inside this joy-filled body of mine as I marvel at the pleasure of my children's company.

And as Thich Nhat Hanh once said, and I paraphrase: *It is wise and loving to consider time with our children as "our time."*

Yes, time with my children, a night like this, is indeed my time. It is one of my enlightened self-interest pursuits.

CHAPTER 16

FIVE STEPS FORWARD, ONE STEP BACK

THE LONGING RETURNS

A near perfect day. It's March 12th, a typical, seasonally warm day in the South: 72 kite-flying degrees. Even the road workers look happy today.

It starts with more "my time" - this time my young son's and my bi-weekly trip to Heavenly Doughnuts. True to its name, I enjoy watching Gabriel bask in doughnut heaven. Then, with a twinge of guilt, I drive him to school and watch him sugar-bounce out of the car and through the school house door. Next stop yoga. Not Thursday's gentle yoga. It's just like I like it when I'm well-rested and wanting a rigorous stretch. I sweat, I pant, and I love the challenge of holding the more difficult postures today: not every day, but today.

Stretched, strengthened, and steady, I head to work. Bam, bam, bam, bam: four relatively easy clients back to back, then back out to play with my adult daughter in the sunshine. We walk around the lakes, and with all the exuberance of a woman in her early twenties, she bubbles on about the events du jour. Then rather than attend an equally strenuous power class like we had planned, we decide to walk accompanied now by her beautiful boyfriend to the Mexican restaurant on LSU's campus. We have Patron margaritas instead. One of the things I appreciate most about her and myself is our ability to remain flexible: tonight's power yoga, fairly traded for Mexican and Margaritas.

We eat, we drink, and we are merry. Claire shares stories about her father and her brother. She shares stories about a co-worker who got naked at a festival after drinking too much. The sun's setting, and I feel glorious. Patron enhances the glory, yes, but the glory was mine before the first sip. What a beautiful morning. What a beautiful day. What a wonderful evening. Everything's going my.....

INCOMING: A text from Ryan.

"Where are you? I need to eat. Are you hungry?"

I reply: "We're at The Mexican place at the North Gates of campus having Patron and fajitas.
You want to join us?"

His response: "Yep. 20 minutes."

At that point I order a top-shelf margarita on the rocks for him. I decide to order myself another. Then minutes later he saunters in with that swag he's taken to art form, and his teammates greet him with enthusiasm. (He plays soccer with Matt, Claire and Cody on a co-ed team. They bond and banter over drinks like good teammates do.)

I'm still enjoying myself. I feel relaxed and easy. Our conversation flows seamlessly as it often does. There's no tension. We've managed, over the last few months, to create a deep friendship out of the ashes of the relationship that was lost. And then it happens. Claire shares something that is part of an inside joke between Ryan and I. We glance at each other at the same time: smiling wryly as two people who hold an inside joke between them do.

Both the glance and the smile last one second too long. And I notice in that fatal extra second that tonight his eyes are devilishly green. When he's shirtless they're grey, but in his hunter green button-down, his eyes become their mesmerizing, Dominican green.

I also see the pain in those same green eyes.

I sense there's a stirring for him tonight. I sense this because I can see it in his gaze. After a five-mile, hard and fast run-walk with Claire, my cheeks are rosy, my skin is glistening, and my hair's blown carelessly around. I let myself indulge in a moment where I remember the compliments he gave me in years past. I let myself remember that when we ran 5Ks together, he'd tell me I'm radiant afterward, and I'd bask in the afterglow of both the run and his admiration. I know I have that look again tonight. I see the sadness deepen as I watch his eyes move from my forehead down to my lips then to the hand that still wears the platinum and diamond ring he gave me the Christmas before the year he left. Becoming self-conscious, I wonder momentarily why I still wear that ring, but truthfully I know. I wear it because that ring holds memories I want to keep close.

I look up again, and I'm suddenly aroused by his beauty, just as I've been regularly, consistently for over a decade. I look away. I look away because there are tears forming in my eyes. The tears are in realization that he's going home to his new lover tonight. She lives very close, and she's waiting for him. And my eyes tear because I know at some point tonight, maybe right now as I write, his hunter green button down will fall to the floor, and his green eyes will turn grey...just for her.

Ohhh...why did the longing have to return? I was doing so well. I hurt. I hurt. I hurt right now.

And then in the middle of this gentle, but immobilizing, pain, my heart cracks open wider. I have a sudden awareness. A delicate French phrase comes to mind: Belle Douleur. Belle Douleur means "sweet sadness," and is also the title of my magnificent goddaughter's book about the life of a beautiful Cajun maiden coming of age on the bayous of Louisiana. The feeling I feel tonight can only be felt when I'm solid enough to allow my heart to remain open to the love that's still there, and to the love that's been lost. And now that I think about it, this feels to me to be a much more inhabitable place than the old protective anger I often feel when he accidentally gets too close.

Belle Douleur – the sweet sadness that comes with the realization that I can only hurt this much, because I've had the courage to love this deeply.

CHAPTER 17
NAMASTE, BITCH

Seven p.m. on a glorious Friday night: I'm meeting one of my best friends, Andy, at The Daily Grind. Andy is part-owner of this hip-and-happening coffee shop, dinette and art gallery in our hip, happening mid-city area. The Daily Grind compliments her well. Andy is as amazing of an artist as she is a gourmet chef. Tonight there's an art exhibit, and her wizardry in the kitchen is an outstanding companion to her wizardry on the easel. Together she, her art and her gourmet treats grace the evening at The Grind.

As I enter the shop, Andy hands me a glass of wine before I even settle in. As she does, she introduces me again to her friend Antoinette. We've met before for a White Light Art Night party at Andy's. I'm immediately drawn to Antoinette. She's bold and stylish and is telling the person behind the counter that she wants more berries in her sangria. The barista is happy to oblige.

As women do, I take a head to toe survey of her apparel. Tonight Antoinette is, as they say, business on the top and party on the bottom. Clearly Ann

Taylor-ish with her white starched fresh rendition of the button-down top, and red hot hoochie mama shorts on the bottom. But the real accent piece is her three-inch red patent leather high heel pumps that pull the outfit together like a nun and a whore might pull off their beloved Monsignor's French Quarter funeral.

I instantaneously connect with Antoinette upon remembering she's a meditation instructor. We chat about spiritual vs. technical meditation. We laugh about it. We order more drinks together. Then she says the thing that I immediately want to print and slap as a bumper sticker on my car, the thing I want to use as my new mantra. The "thing" starts with a meditation joke, and I can't remember now what was so funny, but whatever she says, I laugh out loud in response. Pleased with my laughter, she reaches over, gives me a high five and playfully says, "Namaste, Bitch."

Who could resist falling in love with someone so bold that the words "Namaste" and "Bitch" roll of the tongue together as easily as ice and cream? At some point, she, Andy, and I all agree to leave the gallery. We go out for Thai and sake and end the evening at

Juban's around 10. Juban's is one of our finer restaurants in Baton Rouge: French Quarter in style, the elegant architecture complements the exceptional tastes of the French Cajun cuisine.

Antoinette introduces me to Honey Bourbon Clean: Blanton's Bourbon, no ice. I have to taste it clean, not dirty. Chris, the cute young bartender, graciously pours me way more than an ounce. I've always considered Bourbon the most seductive of all dark alcohols, but after tasting Honey Bourbon straight, I ask Chris to add some crushed ice and a little mint. (Here in the South, we call this drink a Mint Julep.) He asks me if I want him to place the mint whole in the glass, or if I prefer that he crush it with his fingers. I stare deep into his eyes and say, "By all means, Sugar, use your fingers." He nods, smiles and obeys.

Upon delivery of my Julep with top shelf Blanton's Bourbon, I move to the sofa near the fireplace, while Andy and Antoinette stay standing. They're engaged in conversation with each other. And they are engaging to watch as well. Then I begin to watch the men who are watching them. I'm in awe. I'm in awe because both women, femme fatales each in their own right, are in complete command of this New Orleans courtyard-style lounge. They are both gorgeous, bold, and seem to be crystal clear about who they are and what they need. I'm taking notes.

I'm aware that I'm not interested in the men in the room tonight, but more interested in watching these two women be adored by them. They're both in relationships with wonderful men, so neither of them even notice the adoration of the strangers around them, but I do. And as I continue to watch with utter fascination, Antoinette catches me from the corner of her eyes and lifting her glass to me says once again: "Namaste, Bitch." I nod and reply with my own glass held high, "Namaste, Bitch."

Indeed, Namaste, Bitch – a phrase charged with super sexiness, a phrase that speaks into the integral image of both the sacred and the profane. To have one without the other is to live a life without balance. Like Andy and Antoinette, I'm clear I want to dance in both worlds. Those words were a perfect reminder tonight of what is truly enrolling to my spirit: "Namaste" (the god in me, sees the god in you), and "Bitch" (saucy, earthy mama)...yes, perfect tonight.

CHAPTER 18
ALARMING STATISTICS

APRIL 14, 2010

Posting to a married friend on Facebook: *"And I don't want to pretend, there are times when life's been really hard. I've felt the full gestalt of loneliness. There is this very hollow, empty feeling – a cold wind blowing right through the holes in my heart that reminds me that no one currently has me as their top priority – no one, that is, but me. This realization has been the hardest to deal with...realizing that there is no solid partnership that speaks the promise: 'I have your back honey.' I hope, John, you can have a full appreciation of how blessed you are to have that in your life. It's easily taken for granted."*

That's what I wrote to my friend John tonight. I've been wrestling again with that hollow feeling lately – wrestling it down with the same success I would a 10-foot gator from the swamps back home. I can even feel that cold bayou wind blowing right thought the hollow parts of my insides right now – this vulnerable feeling of being completely, solely responsible for my household, for my business, for my budget, and most importantly, for my health and happiness: in essence, my entire well-being.

Having had one mate after another for over four decades (since adolescence to be exact), it's a fairly unfamiliar feeling – this "no one person's got my back" feeling, that is. Every fiber of my being knows this. I feel it deep in the primordial recesses of my soul, deep down in my limbic system.

This primal fear particularly haunts me at the end of a riveting church service. No partner to turn to and say, "Wow, that was amazing." It's also haunting me during the current recession. No industrious man to turn to and ask, "Hey honey, can you slip a few hundred in my bank account to cover those bills?" Nobody home to hand me an empty container and a cold rag for my head on that grueling Friday afternoon when I was poisoned with bad fast food.

I don't like this. I don't want this. And frankly, I refuse to accept this as my lot in life. I think that my Christian, Buddhist and Hindu studies have a lot to offer in many domains, but, as for the notions of surrender and acceptance: *This?* A strong, vocal and voting member of my internal court says, *No way!* I come from a long lineage of tenacious, won't-take-no-for-an-answer pirates and Mediterranean immigrants. We don't give up when the rowing gets hard. We don't give up looking for land when there's no land in sight. We don't give up when the water gets rough. It's deep in my blood to break barriers, refuse to accept limits or adhere to someone else's rules or beliefs when they don't feel right for me.

But, despite my conviction to remedy this partner situation with the support of a loving God, it became profoundly apparent to me last Monday night how on my own I am. It became apparent when my house alarm went off at 1:48am and there was no big, courageous man lying next to me to nudge awake and say, "Go see what that is." To be jolted awake in the middle of the night to the very alarming sound of a house alarm was nothing short of bone-chilling, and a very loud reminder of how alone I really am.

I did manage to have, in the time between calling 911 and waiting the 25 ridiculous minutes it took for the police to arrive, an empowering moment with "myself" that made the whole ordeal worth its cost. I had a coming-into-my-own moment. It happened after huddling in the fetal position for about ten minutes talking with the 911 "Urgent Situation

Dispatcher." Realizing the police weren't in any hurry to rescue me, I grabbed a bat I keep next to my bed and the pepper spray I keep in my nightstand, and said, "Okay, asshole. You want some of me? Well try to come in, 'cause I have some power waiting for you."

As it turns out, the alarm tripped from a low battery and not from a man wanting to batter me. Trauma resolved, dust settling, as I lay my head back down to rest, three deeper insights came into my awareness.

One: When there is no one more capable than me around, I'm capable of shifting, in a matter of seconds, from a helpless damsel in distress, to a kickass and take names defender of myself.

Two: I really want a man beside me so I don't have to kick ass alone.

Three: I'm okay with me for wanting not to have to defend myself alone. It's primal to feel safer in numbers.

And with all that said, not every day is like this. In fact, most days I feel a deepening sense of joy and wholeness (okayness) with being a single woman of fifty. Today however, was not one of those days. Today was a day when the okayness was trumped by the not-okayness. I know that I can ask for support. I have friends who would gladly loan me money. I have friends I could call in the middle of the night. I have friends who would come over just to hand me an empty container and a cold rag for my feverish forehead. But, there is truly no replacing that nearly all-encompassing partner who can do it all without me having to go through the discomfort, the vulnerability and the fears of having to pick up the phone and ask.

So I'm pissy and sullen tonight and challenged a friend on a Facebook chat. (Facebook is my late night companion these recent months.) I took issue with this friend's seemingly shallow quote: "No one can take your self-esteem away, and no one can give it back to you either." I called bullshit on that one. And so, I countered her quote with one that rang much more true for me.

Self-regard is neither created nor destroyed in a vacuum. It takes an unconscious community to destroy it, and a conscious community to help build it back up again.

I do have loyal, loving, "got my back" friends. I know this. I've called on my own well-built community, my Sangha, to help rebuild my self-esteem from its almost mortal wounding in the lost battle to keep my household from burning to the ground.

As I continue to write, I feel sparks igniting — sparks of grateful awareness of the love and lifting of dear ones. But tonight, I'm not with any of them. I'm alone. I'm alone with my emptiness — the emptiness is simmering in the gumbo with the gratitude. I'm alone with my emptiness, my gratitude, my pissiness, my angst, and my keyboard to report it all. And I am also grateful for the feeling that accompanies the loneliness, that even in the loneliest of times, is present. I am alone with me. The observer is always present — that part of me that is so much greater than the sum of my current human parts. The part of me that can see the panoramic view from the wide angle lens, while the human me is stuck looking through the zoom.

So pulling outward and looking wider in this very moment, I realize something. I realize that even with loving friends and family here to support me, some of the work toward deeper self-understanding is mine to do in these very hours alone.

Ah, I just caught a glimmer of warm sunshine peeking through this heavy fog. Yes, I'm alone with me – and I'm blessed with the quality of the company I keep...I'm a pretty damn good companion to myself, or for that matter, a pretty damn good companion – period.

I'm remembering a recent moment with a friend. We were in her living room bantering and drinking Chai Tea, when I made a sharp-edged joke. She has a very good nature and a fairly thick skin, as do I, which allow us to poke playfully at each other's pathologies. So after poking at her OCD, she teases me by dramatically rising, and heading toward the adjoining kitchen.

On her way in, she declares over her shoulder, "That's cold. I'm going into the kitchen to be alone with someone who likes me." (There was no one else in the kitchen but her.) In between the laughter, I managed to yell, "Ohhh...your adoration for yourself is one of the things I love most about you, Casey. I love that you're president of your own fan club." We both laughed out loud, and yet in the midst of that laughter, I could feel this extraordinary expansion in my heart. As I look toward her and see her graceful aura, she is definitely the kind of woman who emanates confidence. And Casey, like me, had a considerable amount of help along the way. I know this, because I'm part of her Sangha.

Here in her home drinking tea, enjoying laughter, it's clear to me that Casey would now prefer to be alone rather than with bad company. And frankly, so would I!

CHAPTER 19
HAPPINESS IS AN ADDRESS

MAY 4, 2010

So I continue to vacillate as I have for a month now, between peaceful solitude and restlessness. I read a quote last Thursday that underscored these emotional fluctuations and spoke right into my current unrest.

The quote read: *"If you are not happy single, you will not be happy married."*

I've been making it my business to become a whole individual without a man. It's hard work, but I'm beginning to believe that it's very important that I do so – Yes, that's what friends and "experts" have advised. According to them (and every bit of literature on the subject of finding one's soul mate), I'm told that my Prince Charming will be riding in on his white horse, not when this damsel is in distress, but when she has slain the dragon on her own, skinned him, and has him cooking over the hearth.

In this scenario, she also had a table set for one – complete with fine china, linens and one spectacular gem-studded crystal goblet for that great bottle of red (or does dragon go better with white?) she's been saving to celebrate her conquest over darkness and her sovereignty over herself.

So I ponder more deeply this matter of happiness. I continue to ponder this while walking with my best friend Sylvia on Saturday evening. I share the quote with her, and immediately she replied in her eloquent, sensual Chilean voice, "Tam-a-rra, we do need to learn to be happy alone." I find myself bristle as she says this. My body stiffens, and my throat tightens in defense of myself. And then I share with her a distinction that I made about myself on Friday.

I told her that by and large I am happy – that happiness is my address. It's not a place I visit. Sadness, and despair, and angst, and resentment, and regret, and frustration and loneliness are places I visit, but happiness, yes happiness is my real address. I know this about myself, because I wake each morning happy to be alive. Even in my darkest days with Ryan, I was grateful for another day, and excited to discover its treasures. It doesn't take much to inspire happiness in me. It can be as simple as the shimmy of a branch when rain is about to descend. Or when my son Gabriel wakes and comes to sit in my lap, shirtless, head of curls all tussled from his long night's sleep. Happiness permeates my daily routine, and happiness is imbued in all the clear and joyful little and big moments of my day.

Happiness is here with me in every moment that I remember to keep my appointment with life – which is becoming more and more of my life's moments these days. Happiness even manages to live in tandem with my loneliness and my grief. I know this, because I made the most marvelous discovery a couple of years back. I discovered that it's possible to be both happy and sad at the same time – I can also experience regret and acceptance for the same situation. For example: I regret going through the anguish and torment Ryan and I put each other through, but I accept that this had to be, in order for our beloved Gabriel, one of our finest works, to be born.

I shared more of my opinions on happiness and mating with Sylvia. I shared with her that I was tired of the contradictory coaching I received by well-meaning gurus and meta-physicists. There was one camp that claimed (as the lady dragon slayer story illustrated) only when you're completely free of the desire for a partner, that the partner will arrive. The story usually goes something like this: "Just when I told myself I'm so happy, I don't care if I ever get married, there's a knock at the door and VOILA! My soul mate appeared at my doorstep disguised as the UPS guy. "

The other camp of relationship coaches advise me to stay completely focused on my target (ideal partner) with unwavering conviction. Ughhh...for over a year, I'd been trying to bunk in both camps, and it wasn't working. And then a fresh breeze in the form of a sane and sensible author came along.

Arielle Ford, author of the book *The Soulmate Secret* that I mentioned earlier, states something entirely different than the other two camps. It resonated with me immediately. She spoke into a truth I knew deep inside of me. The paraphrased truth is thus: I don't have to be happy with the current situation (not having a beloved) to be happy as a person. Rather, I can wait in joyful anticipation; enjoy my life to the fullest while I prepare for his arrival. Finally, a game plan I could live with: expect my beloved man's arrival, but be joyful while I prepare and wait.

What I'm also clear about – and I have a feeling Arielle Ford would agree – is that a person who suffers from depression or profound anxiety will not likely be healed by the introduction of a love interest alone. Perhaps there is a significant mood elevation during the lusty stage of early relationship, but no single person, place or thing has the exclusive power to make us happy. That's mostly our work with a collective effort of supportive, loving others.

Likewise a person who has happiness as his or her internal address can feel sad, angry or anxious (even with a partner), but they always have the navigational tools to return to that safe, happy dwelling place within. I'm pretty clear I'm one of these. So my partners throughout time have contributed to my happiness, enhanced my joy, but have not been responsible for it any more than they have been responsible for my moments of unhappiness.

Going a little further down the rabbit hole, I asked myself, "How do I enjoy being single at 50 while anticipating my partner?" Today, the answer seems abundantly clear: one present moment at a time, one connected moment after another.

Actually, now that I reflect, I think the secret to my

happiness and my salvation during the deepest, darkest moments of my life has been my ability to connect and reconnect deeply with the present moment, which, for me, means to be truly alive and awake to what's happening now – as in right now. Right now, as I'm writing, I can make the conscious choice to be happy. And I just did. I just added one more pearl to my strand of lustrous pearls, pearls in the form of one beautiful experience after another – one connection with friends, with nature, with myself, with loved ones, with a client, with a song, with a piece of art, and with my writing.

One appointment with life after another will be how I'll manage to stay happy, even if by chance – albeit a very small one – my knight does not find his way to the table near the hearth where the dragon is stewing and the wine is rich, red and waiting.

CHAPTER 20
TURNING THE CORNER

MAY 17, 2010

I think I've turned the corner of my life: the Big One. The one that has such a razor sharp, narrow and steep curve that it won't allow me to throw it in park, make a U-turn and reverse; a corner so narrow and steep that it only allows for forward movement into forever. I've finally managed somehow, God only knows how, to feel contentment in being alone. Throughout the earlier part of this year, I've felt contentment in waves, but now it feels more consistent, more integrated into my life. It's been a full month since I've found myself lost in the dark damp hollows of loneliness. I think it lifted when the flowers bloomed.

Ah, yes, the promise of Nature. Spring will always follow winter.

I don't exactly know when it happened. It wasn't a long ordeal – it seems like only yesterday I was fighting it, slaying the dragon of aloneness, tooth, claw and dragon wing. It wasn't a long ordeal – that is, if I don't consider all the self-help books I've read, yoga stretches I've done, seminars and retreats I've attended, psychics I've visited and individual and group work I've participated in these last thirty-five of my fifty years an ordeal. This contentment feels sudden, yet not abrupt. It's more like I just woke up one day this spring and surrendered to being single and, in the process of surrendering, realized I didn't mind it, and not only that, sometimes I even enjoy it! – "it" being myself. I noticed I didn't mind being with me. The loneliness has lifted. And though I continue to wait in joyful anticipation for his arrival, my days and nights are finally free from the burden of grief.

So all the bitching and eye-rolling I did behind the backs of the well-meaning, all the suspicions I had surrounding giving myself permission to stay single for a while, have been replaced with a humble apology to the Universe for not trusting the fifth noble truth: that being single could be of great value to me.

Now, I've always seen the benefits for clients and loved ones, but I didn't see the benefits for myself. As an extreme extrovert, I'm often amazed at how much I love to be alone. I've been alone today for 17 hours writing about being alone. I wasn't afraid to have dinner alone last night, or to run my household or my business alone these last two years. Nor was I afraid to go to a friend's play alone the other night or to my best friend's daughter's wedding alone a few months ago. So one could easily conclude the "give yourself time to be single" rule didn't apply to me. Or so I thought.

Either no one told me the real benefit of being alone, or, if someone did, I ignored it. This would make sense, since much of my life's learning, I learned by doing, not by listening to warnings. And what I discovered in this big time out is that being alone is so much deeper than just getting comfortable and more self-trusting with being alone. The real benefit for me in being alone was to discover, in the absence of a partner there to project all my crap onto, that I have a lot of crap. I have A LOT OF CRAP. And once I stopped flinging it forward into the fan of my primary relationship, I started to notice how much I actually slung onto myself.

In the absence of a partner on whom to blame my difficulties, I began to notice that I blamed myself a great deal of the time. And the way I noticed this is by listening to me talk to myself in the quiet of my moments alone. You see, all of my adult life I've been paying attention to and improving upon how I am in relationship with my mate. But in the absence of a mate, I harnessed the negative energy that was blowing outward, and turned it in on myself. As a consequence (or perhaps benefit), I began to develop an awareness of how stressful at times my relationship was with my own lovely self.

I started to notice how cleverly self-critical I was. I note here that I'm not overtly self-abusive at all. I'm much too educated in these matters to call myself stupid or an idiot or a bitch. The slick and shrewd self-critic that I am slips in the back door and says in her Mother Superior tone, "Wow Tam, it only took you 50 years to figure that one out;" or, "That's okay, Tamyra, don't be too hard on yourself honey. Someday you'll finally grow up and get your act together."

So I passed self-esteem 101 years ago, but I'm discovering that I've been holding myself to such impossibly high standards that no self-respecting person could or would try to measure up to them. I'm beginning to realize that the voice of perfection when turned on one-self says, "You need to be perfect to be worth anything." The voice of perfection when it's turned on other says, "You need to be perfect to be worth anything to me."

I see now that the first part of the work that lay ahead of me is to learn to love the part of me that is such a harsh task master – my inner Miss Savoie, the teacher whose voice I internalized and spoke of in an earlier chapter. Miss Savoie, my second grade teacher who to date is still the harshest, most punitive and shaming teacher I ever had. (And having been a product of Catholic school in the '60s, that's saying a lot.)

Yes, step number one, I need to learn to love my inner slick critic, a woman who can throw such a respectable jab that I never knew what hit me – not, that is, until I felt the warm blood oozing out from the "what hit me" wound. Love her? Not quite impossible, but definitely not your everyday challenge.

Yes, my next task, should I choose to accept, is to learn to be kinder, gentler, and more loving to myself even when I do the opposite of what I intend to do – which, simply put, is to do no harm. To do no harm to myself, to others, and to my planet. But despite my Mother Teresa aspirations, I do inflict harm on myself. I do inflict harm on those I love. I do inflict harm on those I've never met. And I do inflict harm on my beloved planet – mostly unconsciously, but sometimes semi-consciously. And I do this mostly at the hands of my own perfectionism.

So perhaps while trying to find a better way to get through those tougher days, it might behoove me to learn to be gentler on myself. To be gentler because, quite frankly, I can't divorce or file a restraining order on myself like I can an abusive spouse. And I must be making some headway on this self-respect thing, because as I mentioned at the beginning of this chapter, I'm finding deepening enjoyment these days in the company I keep when I'm alone.

CHAPTER 21

A Day Later

June 5, 2010

It's the day before my daughter's twenty-second birthday. We're on our annual pilgrimage to glorious Seaside, Florida — a celestial place where the sand is as white as confectioner's sugar and the water as blue as a 16-year-old's broken heart.

I'm standing on the edge of a rolling surf with big, red-flag-flying storm waves crashing at my knees. It's dusk. I'm deliciously alone. I'm full-to-overflowing with contentment. The momentum has continued to build, and as spring turns into summer, my sense of well-being is blossoming.

Erupting with this exuberant energy, I shout into the wind, "Yes!" I love my life. I love my family, and I am so happy, finally — happy with myself. I stand in the surf a long time. I let the softening glow of the evening sun slip peacefully away behind the horizon. I let this feeling linger — this feeling of being whole; this feeling of being a great lover of myself. I've been gentler on myself these last few weeks. I've been mindful of how I treat myself, and in this moment I'm feeling deliriously and totally okay with me. I don't mind if the right man comes along now or later or much later. I know he will. I feel that deep in my bones, but for today, I'm content. I'm more than content. I'm alive and teaming with possibility.

A day later, still basking in the after-glow, we head west toward home. A day after that, still held in the girth of God's most stellar creation – the gulf, the surf, the breeze, the sand – I check my email. There's a message from someone on my dating service, the same dating service that I'd become terribly disenchanted with months ago. There's a message from someone whose code name is "Itshalffull." I don't understand it, but I'm intrigued, maybe because all the other handles are cheesier than cheddar itself, with unimaginative angles like YOURLASTGUY AND BETTERTHANEVERbob.

"Itshalffull." Hmmm...okay, I'm in. Let's see what this guy's about. At the very least, he's got a little imagination. Click. And, fully expecting my next almost-bald, pot-bellied, rode-fairly hard-caller, I'm stopped dead in my tracks by the likes of Itshalffull. Instantly drawn to his rugged good looks, full head of hair, and the warmth of his smile, I find myself viewing the slide show of other pictures. All favorable pictures thus far: one on a boat, one at his son's high school graduation, one bowling, and one...oh my! *Gulp*. No, it can't be...one of him sitting by a camp fire with a two-seater plane behind him.

The visceral reaction made me swoon, not because I'm into guys with planes, but because my daughter, at the end of the year, told me that she had a vision of me riding off into the sky with a strong, elegantly handsome man. She also told me that she was so sure that this would come true I shouldn't even bother with a man who didn't own his own plane.

This was not good news since my pool of eligibles was already pretty limited. Adding a private plane to the equation was going to make this search more like looking for a pirogue in the middle of the ocean. But this one...hmmm. Look at this one; his profile resonating with phrases such as "looking for an intimate connection," "love the smell of fresh cut grass," and "let me teach you how to fly."

I went to the email he sent to me, and responded with these words: "Hi, my favorite author of all times is a pilot. Richard Bach. He wrote *Jonathan Livingston Seagull* and *Illusions*. Two of my all time favorite books. Have you heard of him? And are you a pilot?"

Itshalffull's (which by the way, if you haven't figured it out already – and I never did until he told me – reads: "It's half full," all strung together by an intriguing specimen of a man whose name is actually Thad) response, and I paraphrase: "I'm very familiar with the author. My father gave me Jonathan Livingston Seagull when I received my pilot's license at 16."

Gulp, followed by a bigger gulp – an auspicious beginning to a very auspicious connection. Laced with yellow bricks – or God Winks, as my daughter would call them – this newly developing connection of only a few weeks has already had several twists and turns, imbued with plots and subplots - clear indications that the Universe has plans.

If the mutual love for Richard Bach was in and of itself not enough, there have been other signposts propelling this connection forward. On our first date, he pulls up to my doorway in a stunning midnight blue convertible BMW. He's just as handsome as his pictures. I'm instantly attracted. I watch his face for signs of mutual attraction. I'm fairly certain it's there. Then I walk to his car and say, "Nice ride," he opens his arms wide and simultaneously gives me a big kiss on the cheek and a warm and openhearted hug. (Of course, we're both Cajuns, so this is not unusual behavior for two Frenchmen, even when meeting for the first time.)

Our first date goes exceptionally well. Chemistry is definitely there. Second date: another amazing evening. We kiss, but he tells me that he's afraid he's going to hurt me. I ignore him, and think to myself he's just projecting his own fear of being hurt onto me. Third date: the words get stronger. "Tamyra, I'm going to hurt you baby." Oh, no. We went from "I'm afraid I'm going to..." to "I'm going to..." I'm a little more alert, but still telling myself that he's just scared and projecting his fears outward. I tell myself this because there's so much synergy between the two us that it's thick enough to cut with a machete.

I tell myself this – that is, until I find out he's not even close to being divorced. In actuality he had only been separated for several months. So the way he tends to move one step closer and two steps back is making more sense now. He's fresh out of a long term relationship with four children at home and all the letting go work yet to do – the same letting go work that I've been struggling with myself over these last few years.

A week later we had a fifth date. The date itself was spectacular. The evening began with a full moon's drive though the sugarcane fields in his BMW with the top down. We kissed in his car. We kissed in his plane. (We didn't fly, but I boarded one of his planes and sat in the pilot's seat.) At the foot of the staircase we kissed in the antebellum home he's restoring, and he tells me that I'm the first girl he kissed there. He qualifies the kiss, saying, "Not bad. Not bad at all." We go driving again into the moonlight, and I stick my arm out of the window and catch the wind with my hand. He looks my way and with a twinkle in his eyes tells me I look like a precious little girl – such music to this 50 year old woman's ears.

At the end of the evening we kiss goodnight and he calls me again in the morning for breakfast. On our way into the restaurant, we accidentally meet his sister. We accidentally met his brother and sister-in-law the night before. He shares with me upon greeting his sister that he got a chill. He says that a chill ran down his spine, because he made a promise to himself a few weeks earlier that he would never introduce anyone to his family until he thought "they were the one."

The date went about as well as a date could go, yet that very afternoon, as he was closing his car door to drive away, and I leaned over to kiss him, he said, "Do you want to know if I'm going on another date?" He just as well have slammed my entire foot in the car door. Actually the pain would have been preferable to the stabbing pain in my heart.

Since that fateful fifth date, we've gone no more than a day without speaking and a very strong bond has formed. The flutter however left my heart right then at the slamming of the car door. For a while I continued to point out the signs, signs that kept streaming in from the Universe that brought us together. His responses were always trivialities like, "Well maybe the Universe is drawing us together so we can read Bach again." Yes, despite the green lights the Universe seemed to be giving us, Thad, "Itshalffull," seemed to believe the glass of our budding connection "ishalfempty."

His resistance was so strong that it should have clearly sent me heading for the hills the first time I felt him riding the breaks. But if overt resistance didn't send me away, this sure should have – he told me recently that he really enjoys my company, but he's just "window shopping" for now.

So why have I not put my Nikes on, laced them tight and said, "Run, Tamyra, run!"? Answer: the signs that still keep coming; the gold bricks that seem to keep laying themselves ahead of me, leading me to take a step closer to the fiery pits of what is clearly hell waiting to happen. Signs like my daughter's vision of my true love and me flying off in his plane together, the meeting of his brother and sister on two separate occasions on the same weekend. The weekend he told me he would not bring anyone to meet his family until he was sure she was the one. Signs like both of us finding blue feathers within days of each other which is significant here, since a blue feather is on the cover of Illusions by Bach (one of our mutual favorite books by our mutual favorite author.) Oh and least I forget, the same blue feather that is also a symbol in Illusions of manifesting our heart's desires.

So what do I do with the signs? Given he's fresh out of a 20-year marriage and just "window shopping?" Clearly continuing to move toward him is no doubt a train wreck waiting to happen. The logical analyst and twenty year veteran of my profession knows this. But the signs. My ever vigilant, fluttering heart wants to know what to do with all the signs?

CHAPTER 22
SIGN POST DEAD END

JULY 28, 2010

Here again I find myself face to face with the familiar sting of disappointment – disappointment in MAN-kind, which for over a decade has been a near and constant companion. I'm bewildered as to why the Universe would give me such clear signposts only to let me crash, unassisted, right into the signposts themselves. I'm bewildered as to why the Universe would tease me this way. If Claire's prophecy about me flying away with a man in an airplane was right, then what? This was my "starter" pilot?

I discovered that Thad and I have "companion wounds." (In my definition, companion wounds means one person's coping mechanisms pair perfectly with the other person's coping mechanisms to create a match made in hell.) So, my romantic connection with Thad withers further with the awareness of our companion wounds and with this subsequent email:

Dear Thad,

I'm cutting you off before you have the chance to do it to me. You're about to do it, so I have to be quicker than you.

I'm aware in this moment (sad and afraid actually) that we are both too badly burned to reach out and avoid hurting each other. I'm afraid we could not possibly be good for each other because we have "companion" wounds...you being tired of being needed, and me being tired of being need-less.

This poem came to me tonight Thad. It's for you:

I build the walls not to keep you away. I build the walls to see if you will hurdle them.

But when I see your bloodied fingers making it over the wall, I just slap another stone on top.

Would you love me if I were a damsel in distress? You could play the brave-hearted knight.

Would you love me if you knew how powerful I really am? I fear not.....

So I hide my fear in the cloak of a peasant girl scholar, while I leave my jewels tucked safely in the fortress.

My apologies for slaying you with my pen, Thad.

Goodnight.

Tamyra 7-25-10

CHAPTER 23
HEAVENLY BETRAYAL

AUGUST 7, 2010

I feel the full on sting of heavenly betrayal as I drive across Lake Pontchartrain at sunset, west bound home on Interstate 10. It's been a week since I wrote that goodbye poem to Thad, and I'm stewing and pondering on it again tonight. The drive and my mood turn to one of my bi-annual fist shaking rants at the Creator. A Southern Baptist friend likes to call these her "Come to Jesus moments."

ALONE ON MY DRIVE, I SHAKE MY FIST AND SHOUT TO THE HEAVENS:

You betrayed me. You DO NOT have my back. I feel forsaken and the brunt of a cruel cosmic joke. A beautiful, sensual, intelligent, soulful pilot – inaccessible to me for anything but a few good weeks for a few good times, a few good emails and texts, and then a lot of "maybes" and "possiblies" that just allowed for enough space in which to drown myself in disappointment. What the hell was that all about? God damn it.

EVENTUALLY AND AS ALWAYS, THE ANGRY RANT,
GIVES WAY TO A PLEA:

Universe, angels, saints, ascendant masters and gurus, Jesus, Mary and Joseph, please take me far enough away from ground zero to show me why you dropped this bomb. I want to trust you again, and I don't right now. I want to trust that your signposts are guiding me on the right path – on a path to gentle, exquisite, heart-pounding, heart-opening True Love...not the painfully familiar heartache that's burned a hole and bunkered down into my fourth chakra.

Please show me that something greater is in preparation, and this was yet another trial run that got me closer. And hear me. I am breaking my cosmic contract to turn good boys into great men...to make them more loving and lovely for the NEXT woman. Yeah, now that I think about it, whether you like it or not, I'm cancelling my contract. Yeah, you heard me, I'm cancelling 'cause I'm getting stuck with this aching heart to mend again and again and again, while they walk away with a new babe, and much improved skills with which to love her.

THEN MORE OUTRAGE:

And don't tell me I read your signposts wrong. You laid yellow bricks this last time with green flags waving all along the way.

Pilot.

Handsome Pilot.

Handsome Pilot who reads Bach.

Handsome Pilot who reads Bach and gives me his copy of A Bridge Across Forever, which is incidentally a story about a lonely pilot who finally meets his soul mate and surrenders his protected heart.

Handsome lonely Pilot who reads Bach, who gives me encouragement through Bach, who is a great father, whose mother painted the very same picture I have hanging on my wall of "Bosque Courtyard," because she is of Bosque descent (who by the way mingled with my pirate ancestry in New Orleans,) and whose brother and sister I met "accidentally," at two different restaurants on the one and only date we had in his home town.

So I feel deceived by your signposts. And don't try to

convince me that I was makin' somethin' out of nothin'...these were not small signs that could have easily been interpreted in a thousand different ways.

THEN THE FINAL ANGRY, HEAT-BROKEN PLEA:

UNIVERSE. DAMN IT. TALK TO ME. I so want to trust that you have my back. I want to know I can trust my intuition, my pounding heart, and your divine orchestration of events. Please reveal your method in this madness. And make it quick, 'cause I'm in a ton of pain here. Anguish born of mistrust in you, and worse, anguish born of mistrust in myself for trusting you. I hate that I read the signs wrong. I hate that I feel led astray. I hate that I don't know right now if I ever even got signs from you in the first place, or if I made all that shit up just to keep hope alive.

CHAPTER 24
SACRED CIRCLE OF FRIENDS

AUGUST 11, 2010

One of the greatest blessings in my life is my Wednesday night spiritual group. I've carefully hand-picked eight individuals to sit in a circle with me and illuminate my life with their collective wisdom. I've had many moments with this group, moments where chills ran up my spine in a knowing that what we were dialoguing about were cutting edge discoveries. Discoveries being generated from our synchronized consciousness, and being sent forth into the great creative field, the field of infinite possibility of the highest vibrational planes.

I consider these individuals, two men and six women, all extremely intelligent, both emotionally and intellectually. Most importantly, I hold them all to be remarkably self-reflective. They are deep-diving spirits with both aptitude and fearlessness. And their fearless pursuit of themselves allows them to excavate their soul's lost treasures, to themselves and to the rest of us who are privileged to witness that level of authenticity.

On this one particular night, Wednesday August 11th, I share my "Come to Jesus" car ride with the members of the group. This eventually inspired and transitions into a conversation about relationship. We began to share, one by one, how we had great fear that we were "pricing ourselves out of the market." I.e., the more work we did, the more authentic we became, the fewer games we were willing to play, the fewer people were out there to play at that level.

At one point in the share, Charles, speaking directly to me, said that what he heard me saying is that I didn't believe that I would have my desire for a true love fulfilled by the Universe. And then he said, "I want to believe, Tam, that if you have a desire like that, the Universe is equipped and willing to deliver it to you. Do you believe it can and will?"

Whew...that question knocked the emotional wind out of me. After catching my breath, I took a few moments to ponder the question, and my eventual answer was raw and honest: "It's not that I don't believe it can, Charles, but I'm just afraid it won't." Charles, looking deeply and lovingly into my eyes continued, "I would be so sad if that were the case, Tam. I'm going to step into the gap of what you long for and what you believe is possible for you, and believe it for you. I'm going to believe that the Universe loves you enough to deliver the desire it put into your heart."

And with that said, I felt a rumbling through my body. My heart cracked open wide because of Charles' deep love for me, and because I knew he was speaking the truth about Heaven's desire to give me the Kingdom: a man who will love me as deeply as I have the ability to love him. And I have a huge ability to love. If I only get back what I'm willing to give, (no more or no less) I know I'll be a very happy woman.

CHAPTER 25
FRIEND ZONE

So after our Wednesday night discussion, and along with my constant companions, Curiosity and Wonder, I've actively engaged myself in the task of tucking Thad safely into the far right end of the friend zone. The connection, the kindred sense of belonging between us, is too deep and wide to cut him loose. Yet I am almost certain he is not the one Charles spoke to me about in group.

Our connection however, is rich and generative. I learn more about myself in discovering him. He discovers more about himself in learning about me. I know now that one of the reasons Thad came into my life was to teach me to have greater patience and compassion for myself. I achieved this by learning to be patient and compassionate with him. We not only have companion wounds, but we have companion character traits. Some of the things Ryan hated most about me – my exaggerative nature, my insecurities, my tendency toward drama – are all traits I see in Thad.

Ryan, in his darker moments, had a tendency of

defining my character by my darkest moments. In doing so, I was often invited to feel all the more insecure. I realized one day how ironic it was that when someone shames us for being insecure, it only drives our insecurities deeper. I remember thinking one day that the right partner would teach me to be compassionate with my insecurities. And by showing compassion the insecurities might very well dissolve.

I have great love for Thad's same qualities that in me drove Ryan insane. And in my love and compassion for Thad, not only did he become more compassionate with himself, but I in turn learned to be more loving and compassionate with myself. In being aware of how much I adored him, I began to wonder what was stopping me from adoring myself?

It was a pivotal moment when I asked myself that question, and realized that I could love myself, like I did him. Thad has endeared himself to me eternally for being so lovable, not despite, but because of his humanity. If there is no other reason for our cosmic connection, that epiphany would have been enough: to have learned that I can love myself not despite, but because of my humanity. I have a feeling I've lived lifetimes trying to learn that lesson.

Yes, Thad and I are kindred spirits. We both have great range in our interests and in our personalities. Yesterday afternoon, for example, I texted him about a psychic experience I had while doing Rieki (Japanese Energy Work.) That same night, I texted him a photo from my five card stud poker game, my glass of wine in the backdrop, and a royal flush in the forefront, and one word describing the picture. "BAM." Yes, we can both be described in a quote (I believe to be written) by Thoreau: "I am man. I am vast. I can be inconsistent."

We're both Libras, the balancing act of the cosmos. When I stay in the ethers too long, I might need junk food, a glass or two of vino, a good poker game and an occasional cigarette. If I stay in the vices too long, I need a day of yoga, meditation, and vegan cuisine. So Thad, like me, is deliciously inconsistent, prone to drama, and exaggerative. At times, we both have great confidence; at other times, great insecurities. It's what I like best about "us." We're both practitioners of the full catastrophe, as Zorba the Greek once called it. And though it now feels fairly certain that Thad's not going to be the great love of my life, he's already set up permanent residence in my heart as a soul mate and fellow seeker of "light," liberty and the pursuit of happiness.

I'll admit that because he's so damn cute, it's difficult to shut the door completely to romantic possibilities. But I'm delighting these days in the waiting for what the Universe has in store. I'm still making my store list. I have twenty-four items at present. Thad fulfills some but not all of them.

I'm grateful to Thad, though. He's taught me many important things over the last few months, none the least of which was to put "available" at the very top of my list. And he is definitely not that. He's also taught me through my patience with him, to be more patient with myself. A lesson which I realize now is well worth any heart ache.

Thank you Universe for taking me far enough from ground zero to learn this truth. All options open and available to me right now, I feel free and happy, content with the notion of divine timing. Well, today at least. Tomorrow? Ehhh, who knows?

CHAPTER 26
RETURN OF THE BOHEMIAN
AUGUST 15, 2010

And speaking of men who are now tucked safely into the far end of the friend zone: Having not seen hide or hair of him in eight months, for two weeks now my Bohemian poet's been pinging on my radar. On several occasions I've thought to email him, and then the mood would pass. I haven't seen him in over eight months, and this is a bit odd since we have mutual friends who are socially active, "about town" types.

I've been enwrapped in a wonderful new adventure at my dear friend's freshly opened and fabulous yoga studio. Each time I visit her new studio I find myself thinking of my poet, perhaps because I introduced my yoga instructor to him, and he then became a consultant to the building of the studio; perhaps because he lived within walking distance; perhaps because he was soon to be coming into my life again – "soon," as in that very next Saturday afternoon.

The first glance I got of him after eight months

without a sighting was while bending over in the ever compromising posture of downward dog. For those that are not familiar with yoga, downward dog is the same position the center is in before he snaps the football - head down, bent forward, legs straight and rear high up in the air. Yep, I'm in downward dog, and I see through my legs behind me – like behind me on the next mat directly behind me – my gorgeous, soulful bohemian man.

Can I tell you what was evoked in seeing him directly behind me, hearing him breath heavily behind me in downward dog? Seriously. To say I never found my "ground" in yoga class that day was not a yoga stretch by any imagination. Breathe, Tamyra. Breathe, my dear.

CHAPTER 27
HINDU DANCE OF RECONCILIATION

To complicate matters, my poet's been putting the hardwood flooring down in my newly rented yoga therapy room. Did I mention earlier that along with being a poet and a journalist, he is a restoration contractor? That means among other things, he uses his hands to restore beautiful old wood as skillfully as he uses them to write poetry.

So my bohemian is planting his energy in the very foundation of my office floor – the place where I'll be offering Zen and Yoga therapy. Now I know why I've been thinking about him every time I walk into the Yoga studio. His energy is everywhere. And since he's going to be everywhere, and in particular underneath me on the floor of my new office while I work – I decided it's time to make peace with my Bohemian.

With that intention firmly planted, the Universe rises. It's Friday afternoon, and here are my two amazing choices (and very revealing of this inconsistent life I described earlier). My two best choices, though I had several other decent offers for the evening, were to go to my godson's title Mixed Martial Arts fight at Harrah's Casino in New Orleans, or to go to what appeared to be a promising evening at the yoga studio for Bollywood – a form of Hindu line dancing. Not able to find anyone to go down with me to New Orleans to watch my godson win his fight, I settled on the Hindu line dance. My one regret was that my godson did win, and I would have loved to have been part of it. But I skipped on over to the Yoga studio with great anticipation of a fabulous evening, and I was not to be disappointed.

There were over 50 people at the line dance festivity, many wearing shimmy wear and beautiful flowing skirts. Having never been to a Bollywood dance event, I had no idea what to wear, so I chose dress jeans and an emerald green ruffled silk shirt. I fit in perfectly (as jeans and a fancy silk shirt have a way of doing). There was a sense of celebration in the air. I felt it immediately and was quickly enrolled. Already anticipating a great evening, who walks in but my fabulous poet and master woodwork restorationist?

I greet him both eagerly and nervously. We chat. We catch us some more, and we walk onto the bamboo hardwood dance/yoga floor. I decide to move to the other side of the room from where he and I had entered. I exhale a little with relief, but before I could get to the bottom of the exhalation, he had bridged the distance between us, saying, "Since we already dance so well together, I figured I would stand next to you." Ahh! I get it now – dance therapy! We are going to heal on the dance floor. Perfect healing modality, given our beginnings last year at this very time: late nights dancing to techno at Oz on Bourbon Street, Jazz on Royal (accent on the 'al'), dancing to Zydeco in the small rural towns on plywood floors, and now we began to stomp our feet and sway our hips to Bollywood. This time we dance on the bamboo floors that master craftsman laid down with his very hands. Yes, we dance the evening away once again, and in turn begin to repair our very soulful-but-interrupted friendship in one of the two activities we synchronize amazingly well in. D a n c e .

CHAPTER 28

LUFFA WITH A HANDLE

Lavender oil from my morning massage still on my back, I'm soaking in a hot sudsy tub, soaking and working steadily to remove the oil's remains. I'm using yoga arm postures to try to reach the difficult crease in the middle of my back when a visual of a man takes form. He's sitting in the tub behind me, dipping a luffa in the water and lathering it with handmade chamomile mandarin soap. He's scrubbing my back in gentle circles tenderly, attentively moving his hands across my back and down. He's delighted to be here. I'm delighted to have him.

I enjoy the pleasure of this fantasy for a few more moments, but eventually discontent sets in, discontent that forms around the real and present frustration of trying to posture myself in ways that reach my entire back. I'm once again reminded that scrubbing massage oil from my own back is at least as difficult as trying to self-apply sun screen to those same areas – except that it's entirely appropriate to ask a friend or one's offspring to apply sunscreen, but somewhat creepy to ask either one to scrub my back while in the tub.

As I continue to fret about how to get the oil from the middle of my back, my discontent turns into longing. I want a handsome partner right now to take a hot sudsy luffa to my back. And it's so apparent to me right now that I don't have one.

Then my next thought is one I offer to my clients: *In the absence of a beloved, what are my options?* Can I ask for help? I've already established that asking friends or relatives for this kind of support is more than a tad bit inappropriate. Can I peacefully accomplish this alone? Certainly I must be able to accomplish this alone, but this one is tricky.

Ah ha! I have a revelation. That is what the handles on luffas were made for – people like me who take their baths and showers alone. I don't have a luffa with a handle on it – never had a need for one until this year. I could buy one. Yes, I can get the oil off with a luffa with a handle. I'll add that to the grocery list.

Seemingly satisfied, I settle down into the tub a little further. I let the warm water touch my lips. I notice my lips moving downward. And then I feel them start to quiver as a lone tear forms around the whites of each eye. I don't want to buy a luffa with a handle on it.

CHAPTER 29
SERENADE OF THE CICADAS

Lavender oil from yesterday morning's massage still in the crease down my back, I awaken gently to the sound of chimes which long ago replaced the jarring buzzer of my alarm. I rise easily and eagerly today with that familiar tug of anticipation sitting, like a puppy, impatiently waiting to be taken for a walk.

I'm aware and grateful this morning that it's rare for me to feel unhappy to wake and start the day. Even in my college days with massive hangover headaches, I couldn't wait to rid myself of the pain, so I could get on with whatever life had planned that day. Even last year, when my painfully broken heart woke me up long before my chimes had a chance to, I opened my eyes with curiosity and wonder for what the day would bring.

Often when I hear my clients speak about the debilitating symptoms of depression or anxiety – symptoms that make it difficult and sometimes impossible to leave the bed – I say a silent prayer of gratitude for my ability to know somewhere beyond the current pain, that this is a day gifted to me. And pausing, I realize I have my beloved mother to thank for that.

My mother's life was definitely not a bed of roses. My father drank heavily for years and her eldest son, my eldest brother, suffered with schizophrenia for years before he died way too young. But despite her daily challenges, I always remember her rising early, before she woke us, to have her coffee and prayer time alone. And after spending quality time in solitude, she would sweetly and softly come into my room and wake me with the words, "Rise and shine, my baby."

I'm 50 now, but when I visit her in New Orleans overnight and need to leave early, I still ask her to wake me, probably because she still wakes me with that old familiar, "Rise and shine, my baby," or some derivative thereof. Perhaps waking to her sweet voice for so many years is why I now prefer the sound of chimes to the irritating buzzing of an unfamiliar and jarring alarm.

So with that familiar feeling of anticipation of another wondrous day, like my mother before me, I brew a cup of Cajun blend coffee and chicory, add a dash of cinnamon with some steamed half and half, and step out to the patio to sit, contemplate and pray.

This morning my mind is soft and open. The alligator wrestling match with my thoughts hasn't yet begun. I'm feeling receptive to my surroundings. I watch the sun rise in between the two houses in front of me, and I feel the breeze moving through my sturdy old oaks, respectable old oaks that have recently weathered the likes of Hurricanes Katrina and Gustav. And as I have a moment with them – a moment of appreciation and admiration for their strength and grace to weather life's great storms and stay standing tall – I hear, perhaps in response to my admiration, the chanting of Cicadas perched invisible to my sight, but intensely apparent to my ears in those same oaks.

I actually thought they were locusts until I later shared my morning experience with a yogi friend. "Cicadas" she said. "Not locusts – Cicadas." But the sound, though I've heard it a thousand times before as locusts, was different today. I heard a few at first, then there were more, then it seemed that all of the Cicadas in all of the oaks were chanting. At one point, they hit a Cicada Crescendo, and then they slowly and softly died down. I sat for a long time, mesmerized by the loveliness of this Cicada Serenade.

Several times I heard the rise and the fall of this

sacred sound, and I began to feel more awake and alive than I could remember. A rush ran down my spine as I got a sense that their chanting was orchestrated just for me. Then a wave of anticipation swept over the front of me, rose through my heart, and planted the sweetness of a smile across my face. There was a vibrating pulse in the air around me as I heard these words from deep within:

"An exciting new adventure is about to begin. The first amazing 50 years are behind you now, and the the best half is yet to come. The Cicadas are here to announce its arrival today. So rejoice and be glad in it."

CHAPTER 30
JUNE CLEAVER PEARLS
WITH A BLACK EYE PATCH

SEPT. 8, 2010

I've spoken before about the amazing group of spirits that meet in my office on the second and fourth Wednesdays of the month: my deep-diving, self-insightful, authentic, open-hearted Sangha.

On this particular Wednesday night and forgetting momentarily about the message I received from the Cicadas, I'm sharing how afraid I am that my cosmic picker is broken. I share how I've asked the Universe, point blank, for specific qualities in my true love, and what shows up instead is a heartbroken, pithy jet pilot who keeps me at a long arm's length with mutual quick-witted sparring and half-hearted truths rather than full-hearted honesty.

There's a moment in group when Adam, after listening silently for some time, said to me, "You don't sound to me like you know what you want, so how can the Universe provide you with something you are unclear about?" And in that instant I felt a bolt of lightning strike me solid, and I heard myself say to myself, "No...no, that's not true. I do know what I want. They just happen to be two very different and mutually exclusive desires."

Unfolding in front of me were two distinctly different images. One image was June Cleaver in pearls with the white picket fence behind her, and the other image was my pirate ancestor with the black eye patch and red bandanna, joyfully, whimsically roaming the seven seas. Roam the seas, as Father Anthony de Mello wrote, "free to be myself, to think my thoughts, indulge my tastes, follow my inclinations, behave in ways that I decide are to my liking."

So I share with Adam and the group the Paradoxical imagery. Then Adam, who is familiar with my recent trials and tribulations and has also been around long enough to remember the struggles with my former husband, says to me, "Well this all makes sense to me, Tam. The Universe is not giving you what you want; it's giving you who you are."

Bam! Second bolt of lightning! This time I'm singed crispy. I realize in the next instant that my pilot with the blunt, arrogant charm is not exactly what I want, but he is exactly what I am: my male twin soul who just purchased a country home in the sweet southern sugarcane fields – sugarcane fields that any respectable white picket fence would love to wrap itself around. But he is also filled with wide-eyed adventure, wanderlust and desire to find his "true love" and faithful companion.

Yes, sounds a lot like me. He is me! Meanwhile, I'm sending the Universe mixed messages, and the Universe, in turn, is sending me me – a person who lacks clarity about whether he wants to live the life of white picket fences or continue to sail the seas in search of greater bounty. (Or is it booty?)

Adam says I can have both, and the group agrees. They all seem to believe that I can have both security and great adventure, but I don't see how I can. Not yet. I don't yet see how I can pull off June Cleaver pearls with a black eye patch, but I want to.

No wait. I intend to!

CHAPTER 31
TERROR VS. REASON

SEPT. 9, 2010

Still feeling dizzy from last night's paradigm shift, I keep repeating to myself, "I'm attracting not what I want, but rather who I am." And I'm growing more and more concerned about how I'm going to manage to find a loyal, stable, secure partner, when I also want swashbuckling adventure? How do I cultivate loyalty, stability and security in my country manor, while remaining free to be myself, indulge my tastes, and do what is to my liking? In my desire for resolution, I did what I often do to sooth, mend and integrate. I write.

I began to type this strange little poem-like dialogue on my computer, hoping for clarity, and by the end of the poem I got some.

Voice of terror: I am so going to get hurt...again.

Voice of reason: Yes, you might honey. But you are pain hearty and quick to rebound. You'll be alright.

Voice of terror: I am going to go off on a new adventure, uncharted territory without a navigational map and never find my way back.

Voice of reason: Yes, you will honey, but you know how to bloom where you're planted. "Lost" will lead you to a new frontier, and that will be your new home until you venture out to get lost again.

Voice of terror: I'll be compromising my values.

Voice of reason: Yes, you will, and you will trade them for new values that are more fitting for the skin you are growing into.

Voice of terror: But, but, but I declared I wanted to be adored and deserving of loyalty and unconditional love.

Voice of reason: Yes, you did declare that. So adore yourself unconditionally, and honor and be loyal to your deepest intention – to grow.

Voice of terror: I'm going to get hurt again because growing almost always hurts.

Voice of reason: Yes, you might, but it only hurts the transient human, not the eternal spirit. And you know, Tamyra Faith, you might consider changing your belief about growth always hurting and consider that growth can also be a deliciously expanding and glorious adventure. It's your choice. Choose the game, and God and his dream team (aka. the entire Universe) will gladly play along. It's called free will!

CHAPTER 32

SELF-TRUST

SEPTEMBER 12, 2010

With my intention firmly planted, I've set sail to discover unchartered territory – to answer the question of how I can pull off June Cleaver pearls with a black eye patch.

Throughout these last few days, snippets of insight bubble up like soft little burps. I'm seeing a vision of my future self, whose real security lies in the knowledge that she's one with the Universe and that nothing can really harm her. I'm seeing a woman whose only real tie is to her intention to be free from the trappings of other's opinions.

Particularly with respect to the part of me that seeks security and stability, I see a woman who knows that financial security is an illusion, and no matter how well padded my bank account, it is no replacement for self-trust – the kind of self-trust that has taught me from all of my life's experiences, no matter how much or how little in my bank account, my children and I have never gone hungry a day in our lives. I've always been a good provider for our collective and individual needs. I have the kind of self-trust that has me feel more secure being my own boss, writing my own paycheck, rather than living in the illusion that a "steady paycheck" that someone else writes to me is more reliable than one I write to myself. I've proven to myself long ago that I'm capable of going out and getting the resources I need to run a successful business and home.

I'm reminded in this moment of a brilliant young geologist and client whom I had many dialogues with on the topic of self-trust. I remember the poignant moment when she shared her self-discovery. "Being self-trusting and independent doesn't mean being totally self-reliant." I agreed, and shared that for me being self-trusting is trusting myself enough to cultivate my very own "village" of loving, honest and caring individuals on whom I can rely.

Zen Master and Nobel Prize nominee Thich Nhat Hanh speaks eloquently and often on this very subject, lovingly calling this concept "Interbeing." Interbeing or interdependence by his definition, is the cultivation of an enlightened community to support our needs – on both a global and personal level.

With respect to the passionate adventurer in love that I am, this is a bit stickier and trickier. Are loyalty and commitment mutually exclusive from freedom to do as my heart desires? Perhaps a re-examination of the concept of loyalty and commitment in relationship is in order here.

Once again, I'm drawn to Father Anthony de Mello's passage in "The Way to Love." For years I've been fascinated with this essay, and for the same amount of years I've had great struggle with it, longing to both give and receive this type of love but not knowing how to offer it to the man in my life.

I'm recognizing that I'm highly capable and willing to give this kind of open-hearted love to my children. And the fruits of my loving them enough to give them great freedom are evidenced by their exuberant and indomitable spirits.

Claire is a liberal, sometimes-vegetarian social worker whose great passions are outreach work in developing nations and working with the elderly. Matt, seventeen months her elder, is a conservative, meat-eating chemical engineer, whose great passions are hunting, rodeo riding, deep sea diving and spear fishing. Gabriel, only nine, but much like de Mello, is already a contemplative who ponders issues that puzzle scholars - Who just the other day and shortly after coming in strong in a triathlon called RocketKidz, said to me, "You know mom, I realize that some of the things I dread doing most, give me the best feeling once I finish them." Stunned by his insight, I in turn shared with him that it took me about 45 years to figure that out.

At times, I blame the possessive Italian side of my family for my difficulties in allowing my partner maximum freedom to indulge his own tastes without being heavily influenced by my own. At other times, I realize few people have ever demonstrated this type of love to their own partners, which makes it another growing edge with few mentors to support me.

Essentially, if I want to charter these waters, I won't have much besides a few great scholarly writings on the subject for a navigational guide. I think the best I can do is choose to set sail with a strong intention as my compass and guide. I intend to have the kind of love with my partner that I effortlessly bestow on my offspring and friends. I intend to leave my partner and myself free to be ourselves, indulge our tastes, follow our own inclinations, and do what is to our liking.

Thank you, Father de Mello, for your illuminating passage. You speak right into June's tenderness and loyalty and my pirates wide eyed sense of adventure. This truly is the WAY to love, and the way to LOVE.

CHAPTER 33

EMBRACING PARADOX

SEPT 15, 2010

I had a moment of clarity yesterday during one of my wrestling matches with Paradox. The questions were flying: do I date someone (loosely speaking) who offers me great adventure, the thrill of the chase, excitement, intense passion, and the fun that goes along with not having a clue as to where the river is going to take me next (aka, Thad)? Or, do I move forward in an effort to satisfy my craving for stability and loyalty in a deeply-loving, committed relationship?

The first sense of clarity came when I recognized that both choices felt, but in actuality might not be, mutually exclusive from the other. On the surface, they were competing commitments, as my mentor Charlie would say. June Cleaver with the pearls and white picket fence? Or my swashbuckling pirate with an eye patch and red bandanna? But if I looked a little further below the surface, was it possible that they could somehow meet in the middle? What would it look like if they did meet in the middle and ended up married? I laughed as I envisioned June waiting inside her white picket fence for her wanderlust pirate to come home for pot roast and mashed potatoes. From where I sat perched on that same picket fence, it seemed like a truly impossible fit.

So I sat with the Paradox some more, and this time a little more clarity came. What if I just accept that for now this feels like a Paradox, simply because I don't yet have the insight to see that it's not? And is it okay if I just sit for awhile, since I'm not yet clear as to how adventure and security can pair well?

Or, what would happen if I just become more accepting of Paradox – to "detach," as it were – and let go of the need to reconcile Paradox at all? What if instead, I just embrace the complexity of my divine and human wants. And though they often feel in opposition to each other, from a wider angle, from a higher level of existence (as Father De Mello's passage suggests) my human as well as divine desires, might not be in opposition at all?

I felt a lifting of something heavy and dense after asking that series of questions. I have no answers, yet I feel lighter and freer somehow. I'm often telling my clients to "live in life's questions more, and seek answers less." So perhaps taking my own advice was working here.

Just giving myself permission not to know, but at the same time to trust that all I need to know will be revealed to me in time feels very liberating to me. I feel a delightfully curious adventure forming in the place where the heaviness just sat. I feel the same feelings I get when I'm about to set sail to a new frontier: curiosity, wonder and hopefulness. I'm beginning to believe that June and my Pirate might just make grand bedfellows after all.

CHAPTER 34

TIBETAN JEWELS

SEPT. 23, 2010

In the Haight-Ashbury district of San Francisco there's a magnificent Tibetan jewelry shop. I visit my god-daughter in the city every fall, and I visit my beloved Tibetan store each time. On Labor Day weekend, I went on my annual pilgrimage down Haight Street and returned to the store. While marveling as usual at all the hand-made pendants, bracelets, worry beads and scarves from Tibet, a mother came in with her beautiful and sparkly five-year-old daughter. Immediately upon walking into the store, the mother gave her daughter a firm instruction: "Look but don't touch." As I heard the conviction in the mother's voice, I felt drawn somehow to their experience.

Time after time as the little girl walked around the store, her eyes would get big and wide and her hands would reach out to touch the beautiful shining object, and the mother would quickly grasp her outstretched little arm and put it down, saying, "Ah, remember, don't touch." As I continued to watch this painful exchange, my heart kept getting fuller. I had an almost overwhelming urge to stop what I was doing, usher the mother out of the store, and take the little girl around the jewelry shop. I wanted to watch her eyes for what attracted her most, take the beautiful object of her attraction and put it in her hand to hold. I wanted to take the bracelets she liked, and the necklaces that drew her in, and put them on her and tell her to prance around the store with them. And then I wanted to tell her that if she so desired she could chose the one that pleased her most.

Meditating this morning, this experience came back to me. I'm realizing that in reading this week's emails from Thad, I am deeply relating to my little girl in the jewelry store.

Last Friday, a gloriously sunny and unseasonably mild day, I traveled down the Bayou to ride Thad's motorcycle through the cane fields of the countryside. The ride was spectacular: sitting behind him, smelling him, touching his shoulders, hips and thighs; the roar of the cycle, the taste of cane on the tip of my tongue, taking in the beauty around me, all my senses fully awake.

Thad and I have become good friends. We talk often, and meet each other for lunch or a visit twice a month. On this day we visited his new homestead. He took me through the house, sharing with me all of his dreams and visions for its restoration. Then as we walked out of the house and prepared to ride back to my car, and as he was strapping my helmet back onto my head, our eyes met, there was a deep gaze, and he reached down and kissed me softly on my surprised-but-welcoming lips. The kiss provoked something deep inside, but not a word was uttered by either of us. We rode off again through the cane fields, both of us I think, happy to be sharing this intimate space with the other.

Later, perhaps a day or two later, by email I shared my experience of my ride with him and my new desire to embrace Paradox. I shared the feelings and desires that arose, and I leaned in a little more and shared that I wanted more experiences with him like our recent ride through the countryside.

His heart-wrenching response, not unexpected, and true to form, was that he "was afraid that would happen" – that, in spending time together, I would begin to want more, and that he is just not going to give me more. I sat for a few days and let myself feel the sting of my own disappointments and desires. Then clarity came once again in a dinner conversation with Vince. After sharing my frustration and sadness with him, Vince, listening deeply as usual, spoke an insight that shed light on my delemma.

He said, "Tam, it sounds to me like Thad has a rule of engagement in place. That in order for him to be willing to have more intimate experiences with you, you have to guarantee him that you wouldn't allow your feelings to deepen in the process. Geez honey, you would have to defy the very nature of an intimate experience to manage that. That's impossible – to connect deeply but promise to keep it light and sim-ple. You would have to be disingenuous to your own desires to accomplish that."

Wow...another Paradox. His observation made so much sense of my confusion about the ride and the feelings that were provoked as a result. If I couldn't guarantee that an experience with him would not deepen my feelings for him, he wasn't willing to engage. I think there are many Paradoxes that can live side by side, but this Paradox – to be invited to have an emotionally intimate experience with someone, but be asked not to feel anything deeper as a result – is truly an irreconcilable one. Yes, as I continue to reflect on the ride, and the parameters Thad set as a result, I feel even more for the little girl in the Tibetan jewelry shop. I am the little girl in the Tibetan jewelry shop. I am seeing clearly in this moment that the parameters of "not getting further emotionally involved" are indeed a prophylactic to the very essence of an intimate experience itself.

My last words to Thad in response to his email: *"Feeling sad but clear about the impossible request that was being made of me, Thad. I see a middle ground where we can let this thing between us either grow or wither organically, not forcing either, but that would have required dialogue and vulnerability. I see incredible opportunities to explore intimacy without attachment to outcome and without detachment from emotion. To be asked to have an intimate experience without a deepening of intimacy just might be an impossible Paradox for this tender-hearted warrior to reconcile."*

Yes, I asked the Universe to help me understand Paradox, and the Universe graciously obliged.

CHAPTER 35
MUSCADINE, ROSES AND INCENSE
OCTOBER 1-2, 2010

As might be expected, when I finally surrender the struggle and invite Paradox to reside with me, sleep with me, eat with me, Paradox no longer remains an impossible bedfellow. It's my 51st year. I've decided to throw myself a party. I've come to love throwing myself parties. Some years ago, after other years of waiting for partners or friends to make a big deal over me, I decided to start making a big deal over myself. This strategy, I'm proud to say, has worked out well.

Eleven of us gather at my home to celebrate, eleven remarkable people. Given the intimate conversation that I enjoy with each of them, I find these particular eleven to be the near perfect number and mix for this evening's gathering. (Twelve people would be my favorite number for a gathering such as this.)

Each of my guests is as enrolling as the next. Everyone has their own unique story of heroism, triumph over tragedy, beating the odds and brave-hearted conquests of their own fears – all gathered tonight by invitation, to celebrate my own brave-hearted, triumphant and sometimes tragic yet fairly amazing life.

Being the newest addition to my group of "intimates," yes, I also invited Thad. (I've finally surrendered the fight toward or away from him, and once again let Paradox remain the undefeated champion.) I think he would have been a perfect fit for number twelve. But several hours before the party, I get a text from him asking me what I was doing. I shared with him eagerly that I was enjoying a birthday lunch with Sylvia. He quickly apologizes for forgetting it was my birthday. He said he thought it was tomorrow. Somewhat annoyed, but not surprised, I texted him back a frown like this :-(. And after a few moments of disappointment, I turned my attention back to my lovely lunch and my equally lovely lunch companion.

So, Thad being the only disappointment of the evening, one by one my friends stream in. I grow more and more exuberant with each new guest's arrival. I should note here that it doesn't take a birthday celebration for me to feel exuberant. My temperament imbued with my high-voltage hard wiring creates an inner environment that is well-suited for frequent bouts of it. And I was already feeling full-to-overflowing with an evening going remarkably well, when I heard the roar of a motorcycle outside my door.

For a second I held onto my delight. What if it wasn't my handsome Cajun Harley-riding airplane pilot? Could it be another friend who has a motorcycle? No, cause I didn't invite any other friends who have motorcycles.

I tentatively go to the door and open it. Just like in the movies, there at my back door stood a mystery man dismounting his bike, while taking his helmet from his head. After a long moment, and helmet off now, I could clearly see that it was Thad. I eagerly bridge the ten feet of distance between us and throw my welcoming arms around him. I kiss him on the cheek, and then with my resolve momentarily forgotten, I indulge an urge to plant a bigger, more enthusiastic kiss upon his lips. I hug him big and tight as I sway from side to side with him while he whisper-sings "Happy Birthday" in my right ear. He doesn't offer an explanation; I don't ask for one. My fantastic birthday party just tipped over the top.

So I'm happy, yes – yet I'm also conscious enough to see that Paradox is still lurking somewhere behind the scenes. Will Thad be expecting me to defy the very nature of the intimate connection we have again? Will he expect me to defy it by being at an intimate gathering with him, and not feel any deeper intimacy for him? Will I ignore the fact that he traveled one-and-a-half hours through Cajun countryside then interstate to get to me, and pretend it's no big deal, and he's no big deal, and my delight in having him with me tonight is no big deal either?

I once again make a conscious choice to let those questions simmer on the back burner, and I take Thad's hand and walk him into my happy little home. I notice he's carrying a bottle of muscadine wine. A muscadine is a honey-sweet grape grown in Louisiana. I decide to have a glass of that delicious vintage and enjoy the bringer of that wine for as long as he'll give himself to me to enjoy.

So, on my birthday night, I embrace Paradox, and Paradox becomes my friend. I enjoy his companionship at my party, and then after the other guests leave, I enjoy him alone on a crisp moonlit Harley ride. He leaves in the quiet hours of early morning.

It's 2 am, and I'm still sitting here, too happy to call it a night, and on the wake of the day of my birth I decide to write till the sun shows up.

I have incense called *Gratitude* burning that I received as a birthday present, a glass of the remaining Madame Muscadine Wine, pink roses on my desk top, and happy to report, I'm enjoying my 51st year immensely. I already know it's going to be a great year...best ever I suspect. No, best ever I declare.

Chapter 36

Explaining the Ineffable

October 7, 2010

A week after my birthday, I discover more super-glue: I'm sitting in a cafe with Thad, once again trying hard not to be too excited about the experience. I don't remember what we're talking about, but there's a moment when I'm looking deeply into his eyes, eyes that endlessly release their gaze before I release mine, but this time held my gaze one second longer than what I suspect is safe for him. And what happened next was astonishing. As I held his gaze, I felt myself transported into what I can only describe as a portal through time, tumbling into layers and layers of lifetimes with Thad. The visual I had was much like the visual I get when I'm in one of those holographic mirrors at the science museum, the ones where the mirrors are cut and connected together in a way that the gazer keeps seeing the self inside the self inside the self until infinity.

And what I saw and felt – all in an instant, a flash of time –was many lifetimes where Thad and I had lied to each other, and the lies always ended in either tragedy or heart-wrenching disconnection. And I had a knowing in that instant that this was the lifetime where we had an opportunity to reach in deeper and be truthful to the point of risking hurt, and hurting the other. And that if we succeeded in being more honest with each other, we could set ourselves free to unimaginable possibilities, possibilities that have not yet been written. We could create – without influence by the Universe, but rather at the cutting edge of the Universe – a place of pure and infinite potential... a true quest into the creative void where things have not yet been destined, but are instead ripe for the picking.

I then try to explain what I just saw to Thad, but the ineffable quality of that vision made it difficult. I tried anyway, cause I knew that this good ole' Cajun boy with a turbo engine for a brain would understand. He would also understand because he's read Bach, and therefore not at all a stranger to mysticism and the unfathomable thrilling direction potential can take.

His response, however, didn't project the understanding I knew he was capable of, and he was glib and dismissive. I called his bluff and shared with him that I knew he knew what I was talking about. He fell silent and serious, and we ended the evening with much smaller talk. But later that night I sent him an email. It read:

Ok, request: When you are up to it, tell me the truth about something that you've resisted telling me the truth about. I'll go first: I've never had an experience with a man that has bewildered me this much, been this unpredictable, but at the same time this psychically connected. Most of the time, I vacillate between trying to tear the superglue off the part of my heart that is attached to you without tearing my heart to shreds in the process, and wanting to stick around for the next amazingly scary adventure. Frankly every time I manage to get a little of the super glue off, I notice there is a bigger glob right underneath. And I'm wondering right now if I'm playing June to your Wanderlust pirate.

CHAPTER 37
BULLETS TO THE HEART
OCTOBER 8, 2010

Just like his charm, his responses are again short, blunt and sarcastic. It's been a couple days since my cosmic cafe experience, since I challenged him to tell me the truth about something which he would usually lie. I want to stay connected. I want to know what's really going on beyond the smokescreen and mirrors, under the layers of sarcasm, humor and protection. I can feel the ocean expanding between my desire to connect and his equal and opposite desire to disconnect – the type of disconnection that always showed up even before he physically leaves.

I push the issue. His texts then become whimsical and way too polite. I push the issue further. I won't be deterred. I'm ready for the truth. The mixed messages I keep getting along with the vision I had on Friday night about our past karma have finally tipped me over the edge. I push one step further, and in Thad's defense, I pushed him hard that time. I balked at what he was telling me, and I triggered him.

I had to push that hard, because I knew he just didn't want to hurt me, and that he would eventually have to. Under his rugged, arrogant exterior, he is, in fact, a gentle spirit. But I also know at this juncture, I need nothing short of complete honesty. So I push him harder still, until I get him in a corner where the truth became the only way out – where telling me the brutal honest truth was the only way to free us both.

So Thad finally accepted my challenge, and he gave me his unbridled, unedited truth; a truth that blazed right through me like bullets to the heart; a truth that had been foretold in my vision at the cafe. And it went something like this:

Thad: Tamyra. Don't make me do this honey. I don't want to hurt you, but I don't have "it" for you Tamyra Faith. I'm enthralled with you darlin', but I just don't have "it" for you.

And then Thad gave me Thad's Top Ten List of reasons he just doesn't have the unmistakable, undeniable, indescribable "it" for me. As I read each one, they felt like bullets from a semi-automatic riffling one after the other into the tender cavity of my chest.

1. "You're not my body type." *BAM.*

2, 3, 4. *BAM, BAM, BAM.*

5. "You are too intense." *BAM.*

6, 7. *BAM. BAM.*

8. I'm afraid I'll never get off your couch.

9. You're too assertive.

10. I can't get my ex-wife out of my life. *BAMMMM.*

Of course being a woman in the middle of her life, the one I heard the loudest, the only one that really infiltrated down to the core of me was number 1. I'm not his body type. I happen to know he likes smaller women. (He shared with me once that his ideal woman is 5'4"-ish and 120 pounds - the height and weight I once was, but am no longer.) It was terrifying to hear as I watch my body transition from the abandoned days of bikinis and sun bathing to the inevitability of the natural aging process itself. It's terrifying because I secretly and sometimes openly fear that I'll be traded in for a newer model once again, then again, and then finally no one even bothers to visit this used lot anymore.

The emails got more aggressive, because even though I asked for the truth, it was a bit much to hear. I was indignant about the whole body type thing. I was indignant particularly because Thad is handsome, but he too is showing the signs of ageing much in the same ways I am. It also doesn't help that he's not the first middle-aged man this year with a widening girth to tell me that he likes his women smaller. I end the email with bold capital letters that say:

How dare you talk about my shape? DON'T ASK FOR ANY MORE THAN YOU HAVE TO OFFER THAD!

That last indignant remark doesn't escape the watchful eye of my conscious observer – even in times when the pain body is in full control, there's always the part of me watching the drama with compassion. I feel the hot, oppressive voice of cynicism eclipsing my over-tenderized heart, and the observer watched it all with great compassion. The cynicism and indignation are wrapping themselves around me, squeezing me tightly, wanting so much to protect me from ever having to deal with being dismissed again.

And even as I feel the all-too-familiar sting of rejection, in the midst of the darkness of abandoned hopes and dreams, somewhere deep inside I can feel a light begin to shine. The more conscious part of me, the benevolent observer, knows when the body softens, and the red hot pain cools, I'm still a warrior of the heart and I will open wide once again. But not now Universe, please don't make me do it right now. Please keep handsome, soulful unavailable men away from me. I'm no longer feeling strong enough to skillfully handle my own insecurities – much less theirs.

CHAPTER 38
ROUNDING THE LAKES

EVENING OF OCTOBER 8, 2010

Feeling fragmented from the emotional aftermath of Thad's last email, I decide to walk around the University Lakes. (Walking, like writing, is another way I clear my head and forge a path forward into deeper self-understanding.) The sun's setting and the work week is over. I'm sad, somewhat tormented, and somewhat peaceful all at the same time. Different parts of me are feeling different emotions.

I feel regret for pushing Thad hard for a better understanding of what he was feeling. I feel anger that he is so culturally contaminated that he put my body type on the very top of his list. I feel peaceful that he was finally honest and I learned about his feelings now rather than later. I feel love for him, because he is such an intriguing and soulful man who I know cares for me deeply. I feel wonder for whether number 10 (he can't get his soon to be ex-wife out of his life) is the real reason for him not having "it" for me, and the other nine reasons were just an offering of his best defense. I feel hopeful –

one step closer to something greater, to finding the one that has "it" for me and I have "it" for him. I feel myself growing into the skin of my own compassion, resilience and optimism.

So, I'm walking the lakes, thinking about the last words Thad wrote to me. In his last email he wrote that he is a better man for having known me, but because he hurt me in the process, he was going to go away forever. I don't believe him when he says he is going away forever. Thad has a dramatic girl side, and he's indulged her with grand exists on several occasions now. On occasion I too favor grand exists, but often find the exit door I used is a revolving one. On more than one occasion I've found myself caught going round and round inside.

So on this sunset stroll, I'm going around the lakes, and I'm also thinking about my body. I want so much to continue to learn to fall in love with "it" with "me" just as I am. I'm thinking about how Thad was here as my twin soul to show me me. His rejection of my body is mirroring the relationship I have at times with my own. There are times when I look in the mirror and I simply see an attractive woman. There are times when I look in the mirror and see the expanded but well proportioned curves of a woman in the middle of her life. But when I hear I'm not the right body type for someone with whom I am smitten, then I look in the mirror and see an overweight, aging single woman.

Once Thad let that out of his well-guarded bag, I let the self-doubt tumble right out of my own. I let the pain of seeing my thinner, tighter body give way to my larger, softer one. And as I watch beautiful young girls round the tight curves of the lake tonight, I mourn my own round tight curves once again. I'm self-conscious tonight, and I'm aware enough to feel sad for myself for feeling self-conscious. And then I realize, because most women are not as shallow as most men, Thad will still be considered handsome enough to get a young woman with tight curves. Perhaps he just knows the balance is in his favor.

I ask myself the question: "Why do men have to be so enamored with beauty and youth?" And in response I hear the reply of my daughter who is both a social worker and a big fan of The Animal Channel: "Natural selection, Mom. To assure the survival of the species, men are going to go for the beautiful younger beasts with healthy reproductive organs for as long as they can." I take a deep breath. She's right – most men will forgo the gifts of our wisdom and our well-seasoned sensuality in favor of the young bitches with healthy reproductive organs. Damn them!

Having just overheard myself say that to myself, I realize that I have work to do. I feel tears well up, and I go deeper still, and at the bottom of the well of emotion, past the anger, I find sadness again – sadness for the loss of possibilities with Thad, and sadness that my body is past its prime and there is nothing I can do to reverse the process.

And checking in deeper still, I find one more emotion – this one, as usual, is hiding under the sadness. It's the mother of all human emotions, the emotion that is clever at hiding under other emotions, and the emotion that has kept us alive on the planet for millions of years. Under the sadness I find the raw, primordial, unmistakable sensation of fear. After discovering its hiding place, I decide to drop in and pay it a visit. I start with a question: "What's going on with you honey?"

Fear's response is quick and honest as it says back to me; *I'm afraid I'll never find a good man that will love me, and feed me and take care of me when I'm old."*

I take a moment to honor fear's honest and vulnerable share, and add from my divine and eternal nature, *"And adore and cherish me, not in spite of, but because of all that I am in the middle of my life."*

Having just felt heard, fear subsides, I hear myself exhale. I feel myself release the angst that accompanied it. I know soon enough angst will be back with her partner fear, but for now I'll gladly take the relief while I have it. Checking in one last time, I notice that relief from fear feels much like, (and might just be) the sensation I associate with peace – peace that graces me with a cease fire from the battles between different parts of myself.

In the last mile around the lakes, I'm able to enjoy peaceful solitude rather than the usual lively debate and sometimes all out war between the voting members of my inner court. Court members who are often in opposition to each other. In this moment the part of me that loves me just the way I am, is winning the jousting match with the part of me that would rather I be different, and I feel free.

CHAPTER 38: PART II
STILL ROUNDING THE LAKES

Moving from introspection to the outer beauty of the world around me, I invite life in once again. I cast my gaze forward and notice a handsome Middle Eastern man jogging by. He has grey hair, a beautiful physique (and probably healthy reproductive organs) and a big, bold smile that he flashes right at me. But before I have a chance to smile back, a beautiful muscular African-American man clips by on his bike and not only flashes a brilliant smile but gives me a big happy hello as well. Then just a little ways behind him, I notice one more man: a tall, lanky, younger Caucasian guy who looks right at me with bright and brilliant eyes. He smiles and nods his head, in a "howdy ma'am" fashion. And suddenly I have an epiphany.

I think all of these men are handsome. They vary greatly in age, they are different races and all have physiques. Which means I have no body type. And if I have no body type, what is it then that I'm attracted to? I think for a minute then realize that I'm attracted to their energy – the connected, present, effervescent energy of all three men that greeted me along the path. This means I'm way more attracted to exuberant, happy, and energetic men than I am their looks.

I feel a burst of joy unbridled from inside of me. Yes, this is good news. This means I'm more attracted to a man's energy than I am any particular look. This is good news because I truly believe that like attracts like, and eventually I'm going to attract a man who loves me most for my energy, as well as the energetic exchange between us both. Yes, this is indeed good news. Suddenly I feel my heart chakra opening to the world around me once again.

I would also like to include here that in the days that followed, I had another epiphany. It occurred while email dialoguing with a friend on the subject of self-image and included the topic I spoke into above about energetic exchange. In particular, the possibility of moving my point of self-reference from my pre-occupation with self-image to an all-encompassing observation of the energetic being that I am – The unified me that is in relationship with all else.

And I wrote:

Dear Carmen,

I'm really seeing today that self-Image doesn't come from the self at all. Self image is primarily composed of what we've been told about ourselves by our parents, by competitively structured institutions (schools, churches and athletics to name a few) and by our peers.

So I asked myself the question recently, "How do we go about "finding ourselves?" As in, finding out who we really are outside of these external influences? You know what I realized in asking? We can't! We cannot live in a vacuum. We've been culturally conditioned to see ourselves competitively (better than, stronger than, holier than or worse than, weaker than, more sinful than...) therefore making it impossible to completely wean ourselves of our collection of contaminated self-beliefs.

And if we cannot find ourselves outside of the conditioning of the world around us, what then is the work? What then is the quest Carmen? Right now my thinking is that the quest quite possibly is to live in the sensations of our being-ness and strive to release our judgments about our experiences, others and our judgments about ourselves.

I think I'm finally jiving with the great contemplatives

like Thoreau, Whitman, Jung, and the Zen philosophers and Yogis who on their own paths discovered that a sense of oneness with everything comes from living in the experience of life rather than judging it.

Wow, when I'm able to do this (release the comparisons and the judgments against myself and others,) I begin to feel the pure essence of being. And the irony is that when I'm living in this place, (in touch with my essence, rather than my judgments and attachments) I think I end up being dearly loved by others simply because I'm so much more present with them.

Ha! Quite the opposite from what we've been taught to believe, huh Carmen? - that if we don't keep a thumb down on our true selves, mind our P's and Q's, no one will want us around. Yes, I do believe that we have all been living a lie. The judge is just another ego-defense here to protect our self-image and it keeps us from connecting with our oneness with everything. The judge, that one particular ego defense is the real trouble maker – not the authentic, uninhibited self as we've been told. The authentic self is much less annoying to ourselves and others because we don't separate ourselves with comparisons – favorable or unfavorable. The uninhibited self, contrary to popular belief and paradoxically, tends to move more consciously, walk more carefully and do less harm, because we are less self-involved and have more time and desire for service to others. Some kind of utopia, huh?

So how do we clear the lens? Perhaps a good first step is to practice making fewer judgments...practice having fewer opinions. Why do I have to have an opinion of myself at all, favorable or unfavorable? In Yoga and Zen philosophy we wouldn't. We would neither compare ourselves favorably or unfavorably. Worry or care about how we are perceived. We would not have a positive or negative attachment to ourselves. We would just appreciate that we exist and have all the sensations of being fully alive- the whole range of sensations from bliss to deep sadness sorts of sensations without labeling them or ourselves. And then, as legend would have it, all of our self-protection would cease to exist, since the ego defenses, as I just mentioned, are there to protect the self-image. And we would look like the Dali Lama with that sweet little innocent grin. At least, as my dear friend Andy Shurr use to say, these are my thoughts today, they could change tomorrow.

And so I could keep expanding - keep growing the edges of love and oneness with others, with the planet and with this organism called Tamyra. Let me see if I can apply this lofty concept to my everyday life Carmen.

Ah yes, I can see how I am expanding just in the way I've been patronizing coffee shops...and I am seeing today how I can keep expanding without the smug superiority I feel at times and shameful inferiority I feel at others.

My coffee shop expansion process might look something like this:

I started out just going to coffee shops and getting a cup of coffee in a throw away cup.

Then I expanded some by listening and learning from others and then taking my own non-plastic, stainless-steel mug so I could help save more trees.

Then I found out about fair trade practices and expanded some more. I began to ask for fair trade coffee to support the industries who promise workers in the coffee bean fields fair wages, which means earning enough money to feed their families.

Then I expanded more and got committed to loving my body enough to want organic foods, and began to asking for organic fair trade coffee.

But I'm seeing my ego is still invested at times. Like the day I went into the coffee shop and handed my environmentally safe stainless-steel thermos to the barista and ask for "organic, fair trade coffee please"....and the person next to me is ordering a regular cup of coffee in a throw away cup, and I feel just a little smug and superior. But then her phone rings and I hear her talking to the vet about her dog. Her voice has great concern and compassion, and I realize in comparison and with a little shame, that I'm not so much of a pet person. I don't treat my pets like I do my kids, and I see that she's more expanded in the area of pet compassion than I.

So today I ask myself, "Who is more expanded? Me or her?" And these thoughts are what immediately arise: "Who cares." "It doesn't matter," "Neither, because it's impossible to measure," is what I'm hearing right now. I might be a little more expanded in coffee drinking, and she in animal care, but we are all expanded in our own ways. It's once again a reminder to stop comparing myself favorably or unfavorably to others, because comparisons separate.

This is frickin' liberating stuff honey! I'm thinking I'd like to hang out here for awhile. And I'm also thinking that I should probably not get too attached to hanging out here for awhile, 'cause if I do, I'll start to judge myself when I can't.

Ahhhhhh, another paradox.

Namaste' Carmen.
(The Goddess in me, recognizes the goddess in you.)

CHAPTER 39
HE WORE A GOOD BLACK HAT

OCTOBER 10, 2010

In the midst of wrestling through a weekend of sadness, I was also preparing a talk. The topic I had chosen months ago was "Aligning Body and Spirit in a Sacred Partnership" and subtitled: "The Spirit is Willing and the Flesh is Strong."

It's my style and my great preference to end my romantic connections with belle douleur (the sweet sadness I spoke of earlier) rather than with an insult in **BOLD CAPS**. As a teacher, as a psychotherapist, as a wannabe Buddha, I wannabe more enlightened than this. I wannabe perpetually graceful in the face of injury. I wanna believe that I'm above lashing out in time of pain. But I'm not. I will, however, say this much to my credit, the credit I've earned as a student of behavioral science, as a student of Zen and Yoga: I did manage to arrest the anger, and talk myself down off the ledge fairly quickly.

So, as is always the case when I give a talk, this week's events wove themselves perfectly into it. I was able to experience fresh, raw internal conflict between the spirit and the flesh, and through my very own breath, re-unite them - deepen the connection between the two. In the end, I'm developing an even deeper trust in my ability to mediate between my spiritual intention to "Do No Harm," and my ego's intention to stay alive.

Much of the time I'm okay with these clashing commitments. I'm equally as thankful for my divine as well as earthly directives. I also know that underneath those competing intentions both my spirit and my flesh want the same thing. They both want to experience peace and connection. Connection assures the mammal a place in the den and increases the chances of survival. A sense of connection also assures the spirit of its cosmic quest – to realize its oneness with everything.

So my ego, bless its heart (an expression we Southern girls use to show an ounce of compassion along with our pound of judgment), tried to accomplish the task in the best way it could: "Perhaps if I point out Thad's own thickening middle, he'll take his gaze off of my own." But the spirit knew even as I knee jerked (or in this case, finger jerked) and clicked the "send" button, that that email was not aligned with my spiritual desires. And though I sent a couple of other mildly hot-headed emails before the night was through, I fell asleep feeling great regret from the misalignment. The cost these days to my dignity is entirely too great to hold too long to flesh-eating, organ-smothering resentment.

Still suffering some, I went to Yoga class yesterday, October 9th, which happened to be John Lennon's birthday. In John's memory, my precious young retro-yogi-hippy Alicia dedicated the class to love and peace, and I dedicated my personal practice to discovering a better way to appease my ego while holding onto my spirit's intention to relieve suffering and do no harm.

As is so often the case, great epiphanies come when I'm in a difficult posture. The difficult posture de jour was Wheel (Urdva Dhanuasana in Sanskrit.) Wheel is my nemesis. Wheel is essentially the pose you hold once you're in a full backbend, or the backbend you hold when you're coming from the ground up into an arc. Wheel is my least favorite pose of all my least favorite poses, yet I found myself eager and wanting to conquer it on Saturday.

So with John Lennon's music and message of peace and love in the background, we are instructed to rise up to an arc in wheel. I do so as usual, and as usual, within seven seconds my wrists begin to ache and my upper arms begin to burn. Rather than surrender to the pain once again, I willfully and stubbornly decide to take a deep breath right from the center of my heart chakra. To my amazement, my chest expanded, and my wrists and arms found new strength. As a result, my arc extended even higher, and I was able to hold Urdva Dhanuasana exponentially longer. Even my yoga instructor commented on the expansion of both the time and the arc of my pose.

In that moment, hanging up-side-down looking like, feeling like a rainbow, I surprise myself. "I'm doing all this with only one intentional breath?" And still hanging in a rainbow colored arc, it hit me – the epiphany. The power of just one deep breath breathed right into the heart chakra. Yes! Of course! Had I taken just one of those breaths before I wrote that insult in bold caps, or at least before I hit send, I would have been able to find a way for my ego to redirect its pain. Perhaps I could have held the pain long enough to find a more skillful way to address it from the cool open spaces of spirit, rather than the hot, dense, anguishing spaces of the flesh.

I think sometimes because the breath is so easy for most of us to take, it is often dismissed as a viable way to do anything quite as lofty as calm the savage beast. But in that moment, hanging upside-down in wheel, blood rushing to my head, I knew, I absolutely knew that one or two deep breaths into the heart could save enormous amounts of unnecessary pain – for myself, for others and for the rest of the world. Imagine the quality of life on earth if everyone took just two good breaths right into the heart before reacting. Imagine all the people... ahh. You did, didn't you, dear Mr. Lennon?

During my talk on Sunday I shared my insights from Yoga the day before. I also managed to muster up the vulnerability to share what prompted the epiphany. The lesson on Sunday and the lesson of the week was aligning Spirit and Body together through the simple yet powerful act of breathing deep into the heart. There is an expression in Yoga that says, "The Spirit rides in on the breath." I never fully understood it until this weekend, but I get it now. I get it from the bottom of my own.

Toward the end of the service, while the cantor was singing an old church hymn, I had another vision. With my eyes wide open, I had a vision of Thad. He was wearing a beautiful grin, and a big black top hat. I saw him dismount his Harley, and lift the top hat off of his head then bend his arm across his waist to bow. As his grin got bigger, I saw him lift his arm and wave his hat up high. I saw myself dressed in a white flowing gown, leap up and mount a white stallion, and as I waved back with my own outstretched arm and my own big grin, I galloped off into the woods.

I knew in that moment he had in part re-appeared in this incarnation to wear, as my friend Antoinette Kleinpeter once said, "A Good Black Hat" – a teacher, friend and kindred spirit, here to teach me to love myself better. He wore a black hat, simply because it was a painful encounter. And it doesn't escape me that both in real life and in my vision, he rode off on a white Harley. In dream interpretation work, a vehicle represents movement, and the color white represents spirit. He came to me so that our souls could expand. Yes, this time he got to wear the good black hat. Perhaps I will in the next. His spirit flew through in the form of a dashing pilot and White

Harley rider, and he taught me that there is a gentle way to hold my spiritual intention even in the midst of the ego's high flames. I suspect he also flew in to teach me that I have more work to do in learning to love my body and the rest of me at this point in my life – loving it (me) just as it is and I am. And if I succeed in doing so, I'll know, because I won't react so strongly next time...well, at least I'll know to take a few deep breaths into my heart before I do.

CHAPTER 40

God grant me the serenity to accept
the things I cannot change,
courage to change the things I can,
and wisdom to know the difference.

GRANT ME THE SERENITY

Though I haven't said this prayer since Catholic school in the 70s, I've been spontaneously saying this prayer all week. It's been erupting from inside of me, much like an air bubble coming to the surface from the depths of the ocean. After saying the prayer for days, I received a call one morning that a deeply beloved college professor of mine had taken his own life. A day later, still in the midst of spontaneously saying the serenity prayer, I attended his funeral. There on the closed bottom half of his casket was a plaque with this same serenity prayer.

I was so struck with the irony between the words on the plaque and how he took his own life – a bullet to his heart – that it didn't even register that it was the same prayer I had been saying for days before.

Later on the afternoon of the funeral, I pulled out of my office parking lot, and as I drove off, I found myself saying it again. This time I realized that the same prayer I have been saying all week was indeed the plaque on my professor's coffin. I made note of the synchronicity, but still very disturbed over his death, I just filed the cosmic coincidence away.

So, Friday night of that same week, I spend a wonderful evening with my beloved friend Sylvia. We go to the organic market, eat a delicious dinner and share some Gelato, then we go to her house and I do laundry there (my washer is broken) and she lovingly folds my clothes while I relax. Then we decide to brew some herbal tea and do a card reading for each other. Sylvia has a deck of fifty angel cards, as do I, and Sylvia is a very powerful card player.

I have confidence in my own abilities to evoke the angels as well. Just recently after telling Thad that I felt like a lioness trying to catch a gazelle and that I was not sure whether to stay in the savanna a little longer, or give up and go hunt an impala instead, I decide to consult my Goddess cards. I pulled a card with a goddess who had two lions sitting on each side of her that said, "Stay strong and don't give up."

Actually I didn't pull the card; it slid out of the deck and hit my knee. I had pulled another card while that one was sliding, and the other card said, "Your manifestation will occur on or near this Goddesses celebration day which is May 1st."

So, yes, we are both adept at pulling cards. I know the reading will be powerful. Magic happens when the two of us summon the angels together. First we do one singular card for her, and it is spot on for what I have been seeing for her lately.

Then I decide to pull one singular card from myself. The question I ask of the angels is: "What do I need to be doing most in my life right now?" I refuse to mention the domain of relationship directly to the angels tonight, because I just don't want to be the girl who's always bugging the angels and saints or querying the psychics about whether she's going to find true love. In the back of my mind, however, the real question is: "What do I need to be doing most in my life right now to reel in an amazing man?"

The card I flip is the Angel of Serenity. And it advised me to remain serene, because God is preparing my greatest good for me now. I smile, and I affirm that I have been working on this serenity thing. Acceptance of what is...peace that God has not forsaken me.

And then it hits me: the serenity card. Wow! I've been saying the Serenity Prayer all week, the serenity prayer shows up at my professor's funeral, and here it is again. And you think that would have been enough to prove to me that the Universe is beckoning me to exhale and relax. But we're having such a good time we decide to do "a spread" of cards, so I put the serenity card back in the deck.

There are several ways you can do a spread. I tell Sylvia I think we should do a month-by-month spread, and I keep seeing the number seven. So we do a seven-month spread for her. The cards unfold beautifully, and give her great hope. Then we go to do mine. I also put down seven cards, but Sylvia tells me that she sees the number eight for me and that I should do eight months. I lay out eight cards. Eight months from now will be May.

I flip the first card up for October: serenity again. I'm blown away. I'm reminded once again to remain serene. Okay, okay, I get it. I'm serene already. Then I go through the other seven. Another beautiful enfoldment of cards, and when I come to the eighth, I flip it over and the card says; "YOUR PRAYERS ARE ANSWERED."

I have no clear concept of what might happen next May, May of 2011. But I've come to trust the cards. I believe the cards are one of many ways that the divine communicates with the open and willing. And I'm working to learn God's way to serenity. I trust that God's mapped out my divine good in clear accordance with what I've asked through my own free will. I know the task at hand, the mission should I choose to accept, is to relax into the process and keep following the sign posts. Yet I still struggle, because such words – "Just relax into it; let go and let God" – are so very easy to say and so very difficult to do.

In order to trust the divine at all, we high energy type A people tend to need celestial road maps and divine navigational tools like labyrinths to pace and cards to shuffle, spread and read. Reflecting, though, on my own tendencies with shuffling and pacing, I remember Sylvia folding my clothes and telling me to just sit and relax while she takes care of me. I know God is asking the same. Sylvia's deep and unconditional love wants only for my great good. Why do I doubt that God is capable of even more? I don't want to doubt. I want to have greater faith. And in this moment I remember that Faith is literally my middle name. Tamyra Faith Bourgeois is the name my parents gave to me and literally means (Tamyra) flexible palm like tree with (Faith) and (Bourgeois) French class.

CHAPTER 41
HIGH MAINTENANCE SELF-LOVE

On every other Tuesday night I facilitate a women's group. Tonight as we round the room with our shares, one of my clients tells the group that she is noticing that all of the self-awareness books that I've suggested she read have one thing in common. They suggest that everything from weight loss, to prosperity, to finding the right man starts with loving herself. So curious, I ask, "How's that going for you, Lynn – learning to love yourself?" In response, and much to everyone's enjoyment, she threw herself back in her chair, went limp and said, "It's exhausting."

The group and I burst into laughter, and then as I leaned over to her to give her a high five, I say as I'm trying to catch my breath, "Yes, no truer words have been spoken in this room. I'm frickin' exhausted trying to love myself too." More laughter from the group – the kind of laughter that comes from deep relating as each woman begins to spontaneously share that they too are exhausting from the trying.

After we settled down a bit, I have another awareness and say, "Yea, I'm such high maintenance self-love, I wear myself out." That time, everyone let out a roar. We're laughing so hard, we have tears in our eyes, and when we finally calm down, I ask Lynn one more question. "What do you do when you feel exhausted from trying to love yourself?" She thought contemplatively for a moment, and then she said, "I soak and sulk." After urging her on, she explains, "You know, I pour myself a glass of wine, put lavender salts in a hot tub, and soak and sulk."

This time I sat quietly in amazement. What a loving thing to do for herself when a woman is completely exhausted from trying to love herself (or everyone else for that matter) — Soak and Sulk.

So, I'm reflecting tonight with a smile still on my face, how there's beauty in this Soak and Sulk philosophy. I'm also reflecting tonight on how exhausting the task of loving myself unconditionally can be. In a certain mood space, like tonight's mood, I find so much humor in our humanity. But from another mood space, I feel sad that self-love is so hard-earned for so many of us. It's the work of a lifetime. It's the work of my lifetime. And what is most difficult is letting go of the judgements I have about myself — the conditional love I give to myself, the impossibly high standards that I hold myself to, the constantly raising the bar if and when I reach a pinnacle of success. I'm tired of the not quite, but sometimes almost, feeling I get when I feel I'm almost good enough. I truly believe that perfectionism is a form of self-abuse. It is the condition where both the slave and the slave driver lie within. Sometimes the root of perfectionism stems from parents demanding we achieve more than they could ever achieve themselves.

What is pleasing to my soul, however, are those transcendental moments, those rare and precious moments when I'm fully conscious of the beautiful glowing being that I am. (Thank you Vince for seeing this in me before I could see it in myself.) My judge and perfectionist both hushed by the beauty of these moments.

They arrive, these moments of glory, unannounced. They arrive sometimes after an exhilarating yoga class, or after a solitary hike in the forest, and sometimes in sharing a sweet and simple moment with my offspring. They are moments of utter timelessness, of deep self-love and reverence for all; moments when I can't imagine life being any more inviting; moments when there is nothing to want or to strive for. Yes moments of deep serenity.

I want more of these moments. Soaking and Sulking and loving on myself even when the self-judgements make the loving difficult.

I have a love-hate relationship with paradox, but to love myself because I can't fully love myself, somehow makes perfect sense.

CHAPTER 42
THE "OUTING" OF ANTI-LOVE

So I want to shed some light tonight on this anti-self-love that permeates my existence. I want to speak the pain out loud. I want to illuminate the darkness. I want to cast light on the things I believe about myself that feel self-abusive. The self-concepts that keep serenity at bay.

I WOULD REEEEAALLLLLY LOVE MYSELF IF I WERE:

1. Always truthful

2. Ten pounds thinner

3. Never too anxious or enthusiastic when I'm smitten by a guy

4. Had a big retirement account

5. Made more and spent less

6. Spent more quality time with my family and less at work

7. Always available when my friends and family need me

8. Tithed more to my church

9. Had a quieter, less distracted mind

10. Baked more homemade cookies

11. Gave more time and money to those less fortunate

12. Was enlightened enough to stop caring if I'm becoming more enlightened

CHAPTER 43
PATHOLOGY TO HUMANITY

In my perpetual effort to learn to better love myself and the world around me, I spend three glorious days, three times a year with 12 to 20 like-minded friends in pursuit of self-understanding and connection. We gather to share our struggles, our glory and our longing for an authentic, unchartered existence. It's called the Integral Course for Living and is facilitated by my mentor, an amazing spirit from Santa Cruz, named Charlie. I've been studying with him since he first visited my church 15 years ago. I've also been studying with these other deep-diving beautiful beings for most of that time as well.

It's All Saints and All Souls Day weekend, perfect timing to excavate my own soul in search of the saint that hides beneath my fortress of protection (aka, sin.) I don't remember what self-revelation I was sharing with the group, but what I do remember is Charlie's very compassionate response. His response, accidentally or perhaps not accidentally, spoke right into the work I've been doing to love and accept myself more deeply. More proof (as if I really needed any) that "life always reveals what I need to know exactly when I need to know it" – which incidentally is a quote from a Louise Hay calendar page that I tore from her calendar that same Halloween weekend to use as a book mark.

So Charlie's profound words to me, words that were directly aligned with my intention for greater self-acceptance were as follows:

Tamyra, self- acceptance is not learning to love yourself despite your pathology. Self-acceptance is loving yourself because of your pathology.

I've heard and written similar words before. I've said to others, "Self-love is leaning to love yourself not despite your humanity but in your humanity." But there was something in the way he used the word pathology that felt liberating to me. I've come a long way in loving my humanity. But my pathology? The very defensive strategies I developed to protect myself growing up in an unpredictable but loving, sometimes tranquil, but sometimes volatile alcoholic home? The same defense mechanisms that after outgrowing the need for them years ago, linger with me still? The same pathologies that have a tendency to wreak havoc on my good intentions to do no harm?

As I write those last words, I begin to feel a small stirring of self-compassion – a gentle softening around the edges of that thick, rusty, armored breast plate. I feel my chest expand. It's expanding as I consider that I'm taking the next step in my own evolution. And now there's a little tightening as well when I also consider that this sounds like a lot of work – to love the parts of me that developed in response to a difficult upbringing. And as I write that last line, I feel self-compassion softening that sensation of self-protection as well. Yes, All Souls and All Saints – the perfect weekend to more fully embrace both the sinner and the saint within. Thank you Charlie.

CHAPTER 44
TRICK OR TREAT
OCT. 31, 2010

As the pattern goes, I stumble onto a new self-revelation, get excited, and then exhale, let go, and settle into the meeting and the weekend a little further. I even do a piece of work by asking my group to support me in my struggle with my growing (pun intended) body issues – body image issues that had grown exponentially since the reading and responding earlier that month to Thad's top ten list.

The support group does a good job reminding me that I'm a beautiful woman with a 51-year-old woman's figure. Again, I'm reminded that I'm well-shaped with ample, perky breasts and soft and curvy hips. I'm voluptuous, and the men in this group, men who love me and are my friends, yet have also learned to speak deep from within their hearts, let me know in no uncertain terms that they appreciate the sensuality of my curves. I'm reminded by them that I wear myself well, and confidently. I dress sensually, accentuating my Mediterranean curves, and they thoroughly appreciate that.

One woman friend tells me that I have the aura of a high priestess. Another female friend tells me I wear myself like a goddess. I find myself owning this once again. I feel beautiful once more. And I know that the work I need to continue to do is to feel beautiful from so deeply inside, that neither Thad nor anyone else can ever rob me of my beauty again.

This is ultimately an inside job. I recognize that the real work, as Charlie offered, is to love myself not in spite of my humanity and pathology, but to love myself with my humanity and pathology: with my 51-year-old curves, and with my 51-year-old habits, and with my 51-year-old wisdom, and with my 51-year-old blindnesses and my 51-year-old depth of character, and with my 51-year-old ability to love and connect deeply. I want to learn to love myself as deeply as I do my children and my dearest friends. And someday perhaps I will find someone who loves me like this too – not despite, but because of everything that I am.

So at the end of the weekend, I leave Lafayette with an even greater desire to take this time in the middle of my life to fall madly in love with myself and madly in love with my deeply rich and rewarding life just as it is and I am now. And again, as the pattern goes, I discover that I'm capable of giving myself the adoring love I have been looking for from others. I "get" this on a level I never have before. I get that the way I want to be loved by others – the way I do love so many others – is how I'm going to learn to love myself.

CHAPTER 45
WAS IT THE WORD OR THE PAPERCLIP?

NOVEMBER 7, 2010

A week's passed since I've felt the urge to text or email Thad. I've found it easier this week to unattach (as opposed to detach.) But something finally shifts. The attachment to not being attached lifts like the pink early morning fog lifts over the bayou, and I want to connect with Thad from a different space. It feels more like Philias – platonic love, and much less like Eros, its lustier cousin. I email Thad from a playful space and say:

"Morning Gou, thought you might like to enjoy a laugh at my expense. I'm at Highland Coffee this morning texting a friend. I have the only thing I could find in my purse, a big blue paperclip right on my frontal lobe area holding my bangs back. I don't have spellcheck on my phone, so I lean over to this college girl, and thinking nothing of it, whisper: "How do you spell 'pagan?' She looked up at the paper chip in my hair, and her eyes got wider (like I had my finger pointed in my pocket saying, "Give me all of your money"). And, without breaking eye contact, she hesitantly and slowly spelled the word pagan for me: 'P- A- G- A- N.' Was it the word or the paperclip?"

Thad's response: "You certainly have an interesting life TFB!!!"I write back: "Everyone has an interesting life Gou. I just report on mine." Later, however, I reflect on his statement and my own reply. "Everyone has an interesting life." Not everyone however thinks they do. I don't believe it's what happens in our life that determines whether it's rich or not, but rather it's how we experience it. Many people might have had that same experience at Highland Coffee and never considered it worth mentioning, but the author in me is always perched patiently waiting to write.

As I consider this matter further, I hear myself say to myself in my head: My life is a work of art. It is its own book of poetry.

As I hear myself saying that, I smile. Perhaps that's why my "default" face (the face we wear when no one's looking) is a smile. I smile because I know I have a wonderful life. One of the great advantages of being a writer (loving to write) is that I am always an eye-witness to what's happening to me – both my internal world and my external world. I'm a vigilant witness of my life as it unfolds; a front row spectator with a season pass. And as a result, I'm in awe in the very same way I'm in awe with the lives of those around me. Strange how when I'm not busy toiling away at the work of accepting myself, I'm often sitting in wonder of it all. I felt wonder and awe when I walked out of Highland Coffee after having that short, rich and amusing exchange.

Yes, my life is a work of art. It is its own book of poetry, an illustrious string of pearl-like vignettes. And I recall a poem by Frost on this very subject. *"No tears in the writer, no tears in the reader. No surprise for the writer, no surprise for the reader."*

CHAPTER 46
SUGARLAND PLANTATION

EMAILED TO THAD – NOVEMBER 9, 2010

Just checking in on you, Gou. Your first night in your new home, your beautiful plantation home. You've come such a long way in such a short time. I'm so happy to have been with you from the ground floor of this project. My heart is opened so wide tonight, as I think of how this project, now your homestead, is helping you to heal.

I wrote a lot on my book tonight. Only 5,000 words to go. How do you eat an elephant? One bite at a time. How do you write a book? One life experience at a time. It's sort of strange, this memoir thing. Not knowing how the book will end. Lots of loose ends to tie up or not tie up. Lots of balls in the air (Is that the expression?)

So if I write just one more chapter about my fateful meeting with you, I think that I shall conclude that there were in fact signposts from the Universe – clear and undeniable signs urging us into a deeper connection. And God gives us what we need, but not always in the way we think we need it. I'm happy to be your friend Thad. No plane to sail off with you in anymore. You sold them so you could renovate your estate.

Night, Honey. Sleep with the happy spirits that are dancing in Sugar Land tonight, knowing you are there to restore that place to its loveliness once again. Your life is a fairy tale Gou. And so is mine. Beautiful stories. Perhaps someday you will write your own.

Love, Tamyra

And with that written, I felt a sense of near unexplainable completion of a divine assignment. In my mind's eye, I tucked Thad gently into his antique four post bed, kissed him on the forehead and bid him a sweet ado.

The mood and the letter were the softest and sweetest I'd shared with Thad. I'm reminded of a poem by an unknown author:

People come into your life for a reason, a season or a lifetime. When you know which one it is, you will know what to do for that person. When someone is in your life for a reason, it is usually to meet a need you have expressed. They have come to assist you through a difficulty, to provide you with guidance and support, to aid you physically, emotionally or spiritually.

CHAPTER 47
ANOTHER PARADOX

I come unhinged every time I hear someone say or read about someone who found their true love shortly after they'd completely given up trying to find them. My friend Mitch spoke those very words just the other day while sharing how wonderful it feels to have recently married the woman of his dreams. His exact words: "Just when I said I love being alone, and I didn't care anymore if I ever found someone, I walked into her diner, took one look at her, and knew she was the one."

Can I tell you how crazy this is to me? Seriously...let me try to get this straight. If I can be like Mitch and just do the work I need to do to get to the point where I could care less whether I have a partner or not, then my true love will finally appear? Really? Grrrrrr.

So I'm still trying hard to surrender to the paradox of loving myself and my life so deeply that I won't need to need anyone any longer. What about the longing in my heart, the desire for my true love? On one hand, I believe that Spirit puts desire in our hearts so that we can co-create the ever-expanding Universe. On the other hand I know that I'll be most attractive to an emotionally healthy person, if I too am emotionally healthy enough to love my life and myself exactly as I am now.

And I'm wondering right now what happened to that woman in the surf last June? The one who thought that life was perfect just as it was. The answer comes quickly. She met with the scoundrel paradox again, and they sparred. I want to reconcile this paradox. I want to weave my deep desire for a partner with which to share my happy and amazing life with my equal desire to embrace myself and my life just as I am and it is now.

Presently, I've decided just to hang out with paradox. Chill with it, bed with it, and maybe even embrace it. Checking in I have a full-to-overflowing life. I am deeply blessed with three magnificent children, a loving supportive mother and close relatives. I have cultivated some of the most alive and conscious friendships on the planet. I have a fantastic career as a counselor with an office manager who manages my business as if it were her own. I also have two other careers as a writer and teacher which

I adore, and a collection of hobbies and interests that make having to choose between them on any given day (Yoga, antique shopping, biking or rollerblading?) yet another one of those high-class problems.

Oh, yes, and I certainly can't forget to count among my blessings my great physical health and my good emotional health. (That's if I don't consider the perils of menopause a disorder or disease.) And, and...there is still that one missing piece. I am wholeheartedly willing to admit it too. I want that amazing man with all those qualities on my list with which to share it all.

God, loving Universe, Holy Spirit, Jesus, Mary and Joseph, St. Agnes (patron saint of relationships,) all the other Angels and Saints, Spirit Guides, Ascended Ancestors and Yogis who just might care;

Guide him to me. Will ya?

CHAPTER 48
DIVING DEEPER

NOVEMBER 20, 2010

There is only one profession man sexier to me than an airplane pilot, and that's the gusty, virility-on-steroids profession of diving.

It's the beginning of the holiday season. I'm attending White Light Art Night with friends. It's an evening of art, food and live entertainment in the charming mid-city area of Baton Rouge. White lights strung across the collective menagerie of antique and art galleries; relaxed, unpretentious yet cultured – how I like my nights, and how I like my friends.

I'm standing in the town center readying myself to meet my dive buddy – Paul. I like the name Paul. It's so important to me to like to speak a name. He's a diver by profession, but at this stage of his career, he's the person an oil company hires to resurrect their storm torn rigs after a hurricane or cap their careless leaks at the bottom of the ocean. He's the project coordinator of these multi-million dollar rig rescue missions – not just sexy, but super sexy. And with Katrina, Rita, Ike and other hurricanes over the last half decade, he is also a very busy man.

So we've been emailing for weeks now, and I've been resisting meeting him – not anything to do with him. I immediately liked this guy. He's authentic, funny, strong, and by the looks of his pictures, very handsome. The resistance is all about me. Since my apocalyptic clash with Thad's Top Ten List, I have sadly and notably lost some of my moxie. I'm afraid I'll be too heavy and too strong. So I've dragged my feet, and declined several invitations to meet him. But Paul has been persistent – not in an annoying way, but in a firm, commanding and confident way. He's already assured me that he's not afraid of strong women. I want to believe him. I've warned him that I have a "Mediterranean" figure – not fat, but ample and curvy. He doesn't seem to flinch.

Finally I decide to put him through the litmus test. If he really doesn't mind strong and curvy women, then let's see how he feels about meeting me for the first time at a cultural event, with a group of my greatest friends and allies surrounding me. If that doesn't intimidate him, then he'll score enough points to move up a space in this crazy and dangerous game of computer dating. And it's worth noting here that this was not a conscious litmus test. I needed to be surrounded by friends for our first meeting. I was just in that space. It's only in hindsight that I can see it was indeed a litmus test, and he passed beautifully.

Somewhat to my surprise, but not completely to my amazement, he accepts the invitation to meet my friends and me at White Light Night. I'm impressed. He doesn't know his way around town, and parking is atrocious, so I offer to have him drive up to Andy's coffee shop and art gallery in the town square. I'll then get in the car with him and we'll find a parking space together.

So I'm standing in the middle of the town square next to its centerpiece, (a large, white, contemporary tower,) and his massive blue Chevy truck slows down. Much to my surprise, I'm calm, excited and curious. I don't have the usual anxious tummy tonight, just the sweet tingling of excited little butterflies.

He rolls down his window, and I say "Paul?" He opens the passenger door, and as if I've done this a thousand times before, using the kick board, I catapult myself upward, and take a quantum leap into the passenger seat of his tall and massive vehicle. Hummmm. Yea.

As my rear lands in the soft cloth seat, even before saying hello, I begin to give him directions for parking. There are cars piling up behind us, so there's urgency to our parking mission. After a couple of minutes of trying to negotiate parking spaces, we find one. We park, and I realize I've not even taken a good look at him or said hello. As I go to lower myself from the vehicle he's already there by my side. And with his hand extended in a gesture to usher me down, I take it, lower myself, release my hand, and then extend my hand again. This time for a handshake, as I laugh out loud, and say, "Hello Paul. Nice to meet you."

It's fairly dark, but I can see that he's terribly handsome, and tall. Aryan with a full head of dark blond hair, what I think to be hazel eyes, a strong chiseled jaw and fair but tanned skin. Though in his late forties, he still has the physique of an athlete, because he is one. He's built like a quarter back, and track star, because he was one. I highly suspect he's got looks that most women would find attractive – as was evidenced by a remark that a Dominican friend who was with me that night made upon meeting him;

"Wow" she said with surprise in her voice, "I don't even like white men, and I still think he's hot."

There's an instant playfulness and familiarity between us that would deny the truth about us meeting in that moment for the very first time. Perhaps it was our few weeks of shared email communications, telephone calls and pictures of ourselves and our children. Perhaps it is as Bach said, "Your friends will know you better in the first minute you meet than your acquaintances will know you in a thousand years." Regardless, I feel playful, I feel calm, I feel excited, and I feel curious. And I'm quite impressed that as he crosses the street and meets my group of friends, he exudes confidence, friendliness and command of himself in the situation...... ah, Alpha-ness.

Like his emails and our phone conversations, he's playful and bouncy in a Tigger-like way. Yet he is also strong and solid. I automatically feel safe with him. I already know I could walk down a dimly lit alley in The French Quarter with this tall commanding fellow. He moves up a few squared with this too. We enjoy a really good evening with my friends. They like him, because he's instantly likable, because he's warm, kind, personable and an interesting and curious conversationalist. More squares.

At the end of the evening we go back to his truck, and he takes me to my SUV. We spend a few minutes talking in the parking lot, and as we say goodnight, I reach to give him a hug, and he reaches in to give me a quick peck on the lips. The evening feels complete. He's made it up several squares tonight in the treacherous game of mid-life on line dating. I drive off into the evening already knowing he's going to call again. I don't think he minds my power or my size. He drives a big virile Chevy truck for Christ sake, and left footprints on the bottom of the ocean. Of course he doesn't?

CHAPTER 49
Coming Unhinged

The last two men I dated both happened to be among other things, restoration carpenters with great abilities. Both visited my home fairly frequently and promised to fix my kitchen cabinet door. This is important for me to note here, because every time I thought to remind either of them, and every time I've thought to hire someone to put the cabinet door back on its hinges, I've stopped myself with this thought;

"No the door has to stay off, because that is how I'm going to beckon my new love. He'll come into my kitchen, and not only notice that it's off the hinges, not only give lip service to fixing it, but will show up with tools in hand and get the job done."

And over time, I kept looking at the cabinet door, and saying this over and over to myself. *"I will know my new love because he will be the one to fix my cabinet door without me even having to ask him."*

The door is solid now. I'm the one who is unhinged. Tears fill the backs of my eyes. The Universe is a truly remarkable place, and tonight I'm a grateful inhabitant. Paul put my cabinet door solidly back onto its hinges. Just as I knew he would. Paul noted the door the very first time he came into my kitchen, and on his very next visit to my home, just as I foresaw, arrived with his toolbox in hand, and perhaps not effortlessly, but happily fixed it.

Earlier that night, as I prepared an herb salad with feta, cranberries and tomatoes at the sink, I couldn't stop turning around to look at him. I'm a little in shock, a little in overwhelm, but I have a full, full heart as I watch him fix the cabinet. In between tears I have a huge revelation. The plane and the pilot were Claire's dream - Claire's vision for me. Beckoning my love with my unhinged cabinet door was my own.

CHAPTER 50
FULL TO OVERFLOWING

The next morning he replaced my wobbly bidet, at noon we met my daughter for lunch, that evening we shared stories and good conversation by the light and warmth of a crackling fire. Along with a full and happy heart, there was also a heaviness looming in anticipation of his imminent departure. I was already missing him before he had even gone.

He woke at 3:30am on a cold mid-December Thursday morning to go off shore for what might be the remainder of the holiday season. I woke with him and fixed a thermos of coffee for his drive to the heliport that would transport him sixty miles into the deep waters of the Gulf of Mexico. I have tears in my eyes as he holds me and kisses me, telling me he's going to make sure that all the young divers come home for the holidays safe and sound to their loves ones. This speaks clearly into the man that's stealing my heart, and this is exactly why he is. He has great capacity to care for the needs of others, and it permeates everything he does and everything he is.

I went back to bed for a few hours longer, then

woke at my usual time and left for yoga. Sad to see him go, but deeply satisfied and happy for this connection, I find myself at the end of yoga class, the "savasana" part, glowing and humming with primordial well-being. This feeling is not the giddy, silly, "the colors are so much brighter" feeling of new love. It does encompass that, but this feeling is much deeper as well.

Typically and after an hour of soft and slow moving yoga, I'm ready to pop up and proceed with exuberance into the day. Today however, I want to just lay here on my mat and savor this gentle, glowing space. I indulge the desire. One by one, the other participants leave the room, and I remain. I continue to feel an exquisite humming inside my body. I feel full to overflowing. There's no anxiety, there's no sense of urgency, there's no to do list nudging me to get up and get moving.

Curious, I ask myself: "What is this feeling? It's so unfamiliar?" And as I sit there quietly in this grace filled space, a full hearted sense of wellbeing spills over and out of me. I sit a little long and eventually hear the answer. *"This is the feeling of being deeply cared for. The feeling of being in a connected experience with someone who is as interested in my well-being as he is his own.*

I lay there for perhaps 15 minutes longer, not wanting to move, but knowing that I can, and the feeling will linger anyway.

CHAPTER 51
FIREWORKS AND ILLUMINATION
MIDNIGHT 2011

I hear fireworks in the distance. It's midnight, January 1, 2011. I've been writing for exactly one year. It's hard to believe I began this journey from a dark, damp empty place, because I feel luminous, warm and full tonight.

I'm aware of the dramatic way I just described the early days of my mid-life adventure... "Dark, damp and empty." Clearly not a true description of my existence back then, but like a good author should, I use drama for effect. I use drama to drive home my point. I've had innumerous clients over the years share with me that they stay in bad relationships to avoid that same dark, damp, empty nightmare scenario... They willingly admit, like the ever glamorous Za Za Gabor once did on a TV talk show I saw in my impressionable youth, that "A bad man is better than no man at all."

Being fair to myself, I've had several poignant dark, damp empty nights this last year. I've written about a couple of them here. But in equal fairness to myself, not one of those nights lived up to the great fears I imagined while hanging onto the relationship that was destined to end. None of those nights left me chilled to the bone and incapacitated like I had feared. But before Ryan left, I was just as terrified as the next person of that very thing happening.

I remember the day about three years ago when terror coursed through my veins as I sat and listened to an acquaintance describe one of her first nights alone. She described the night that she discovered that her husband, (who had left her a few weeks prior,) was now reconnected with his high-school sweetheart who he found on a social network some months back. Her pain seemed cataclysmic to me, as she shared that upon hearing the news, she collapsed onto her cold tiled bathroom floor into a fetal position and cried and wailed for what she believed to be the better part of that entire night and remained on that very same floor throughout the next day. She said had it not been for her brother's arrival, who had been trying to contact her for over 24 hours, she's not sure how long she would have stayed in that near catatonic state. Remembering that day vividly, my friend shared that her brother, upon finding her there, peeled her near lifeless body off the floor, scooped her up, and brought her to the emergency room for mental health treatment where she stayed for several days.

I remember being deeply traumatized by her story, because I had already seen signs that Ryan was readying himself to leave. This was a true life nightmare, a fantasy scenario many of us have played out in our heads. We play out our own versions of this scenario over and over again, and frighten ourselves into staying longer and working harder to appease our ill-fitted partnerships.

But shortly after my final parting with Ryan, I realized this was not going to happen. Only three weeks after a wonderful family trip to Florida for the Fourth of July and while visiting my dearest friends in Denver, I discovered that Ryan went to a friend's 40th birthday party with a new companion. But I never became catatonic over the news or even close to that. In fact, now that I think about it, I did the complete opposite. The day after receiving the news I packed a backpack, packed my offspring and friends, drove up to Leadville and hiked up to the Continental Divide. I had the energy to hike that day, no doubt for a lot of reasons, but perhaps the greatest of which is the fact that I don't have a serious mental diagnosis like my acquaintance who laid near motionless with pain for almost 24 hours. I'm a fairly emotionally healthy woman, who knew it would help right out of the starting gate to keep myself active and engaged with people I love dearly in an activity I truly cherish.

So early on, I stumbled onto the "magic formula" for coming to terms with those dark, damp nights. I took to the business of designing an existence that transcended the darkness. I should also say here that one of the models I used in designing a new, vibrant and deeply connected existence is my mother's life after losing my father at the same exact age I am now.

Mind you, it's no picnic - this resurrection process. The first few weeks are definitely the all time worst part of being alone. Every minute of those first days are ripe for a reminder of what was loss. And within those days, there are many small dull moments of pain that take our breath away and stop us in our tracks, as well as many big waves of grief that knock us completely off our feet. Paul calls those waves in the Gulf Rogue Waves. He says they come out of nowhere, and rattle, rock and roll everything on the dive boats. Our big moments of grief also come out of nowhere and like the Rogue Waves they rattle, rock and roll us over as well.

Those are often reminder moments of the precious ordinary times we spent with our beloved ones before we or they left. Yes, those memories knock the wind right out of us. Sunday morning coffee and newspaper on the patio, Thursday night's favorite TV show watched together on the couch - All the traditions of time and the rituals that we built together gone now. Whenever we round the corner and find ourselves face to face with one of these times, the hollowness can be overwhelming. That haunting empty space right next to us and inside of us flattens us until we can pick ourselves up, dust ourselves off and brace ourselves to encounter the next one.

And the panacea for this deep grief is to first honor those empty spaces. Breathe into them and allow ourselves to tolerate rather than resist them. And as we embrace them, acknowledge the precious memories as well as our great loss - La Belle Douleur- The sweetness in the sadness. And then when energy and time permit, which is shorter for some and longer for others, begin to fill those empty spaces with new life giving adventures.

What I did to replace my Sunday morning coffee and newspaper ritual was to join a spiritual study group that met at my church before Sunday service. It took a few weeks for the sting of our lost coffee and newspaper ritual to dissipate, but it was not very long before I rose eagerly on Sunday morning, and felt a new kind of excitement in joining my church friends for coffee and spiritual conversation.

Friday nights after work were particularly haunting for me, since Gabriel, my socialite of a son almost always has his dance card full. So it took no longer than two intense Friday nights alone, for me to create a low maintenance dinner club with Friends. I put out a Facebook post to some of my cool, married and single friends and shared that I would like to have ongoing dinner every other Friday. I chose the first restaurant, participation was outstanding, and over time the participation dropped off. Dinner night was then traded for a conversation group that meets at the home of a gracious friend.

So one ritual at a time, I began to "plug all the holes" as I like to call them, and designed new activities that were in line with my evolving, expanding self. On Sunday nights, a night Ryan always has

Gabriel, I hosted a meditation group at my favorite Yoga studio. Eventually I got so comfortable being alone, that I decided to cancel the meditation group, in favor of Sunday becoming a solitary evening where I pampered myself with essential oils, read spiritually uplifting books, prepared for the upcoming week, and went to bed early.

The real work for me in transitioning successfully from a partnership to singlehood, was to become aware of the bewitching hours when I needed support most. I did a combination of joining existing groups and creating my own. (Dinner, meditation, spiritual studies, walks and bike rides, art galleries and antiquing with friends.) And as I became more comfortable with solitude, I pulled back on some of those activities in favor of enjoying the pleasure of being alone.

I watched my mother do this, and at the age of 74, I hold, as I mentioned earlier, that she has a remarkable balance of alone time, work, and family and friend time. Though I appreciate that some of us need more solitary time to grieve, I hopped right up the day Ryan left and made plans with friends for that evening. I filled my own dance card as best I could, and plugged the holes one by one. And yes, as I just mentioned, eventually became more peaceful with myself, and my early hectic social schedule subsided some.

Perhaps the worst for me was learning to sleep alone. I have never liked sleeping alone, so this was extremely difficult. Even though I had an exquisitely decorated girl's room in my large ranch home growing up, I usually ended up sleeping in the sweaty bunk room at night with my two younger brothers. And for the first three or four months after Ryan left, I slept with the bathroom light on, and the door of the bath wide opened, the security alarm on, my bedroom door locked and a bat and can full of mace next to my bed.

I'm happy to report that today I only need a nightlight, albeit a very bright nightlight, and I don't remember what I did with that can of mace. The bat is further away from the bed now and I sleep, for the most part, peacefully through the night. Tonight however I'm not sleeping alone. I find myself this New Years Eve writing the final chapters of my memoirs from a peaceful and illuminated space in the warm, cozy, brightly lit home of my wonderful boyfriend.

Morning of January 1, 2011

I awoke this morning to finish the chapter I began last night. I'm putting to rest an extraordinary year of pain and pleasure, joy and woe. While safely tucked within his arms, I fell asleep last night to the sound of Paul's beating heart, and the expanded feeling of my own. With my head on his chest and my neck nestled in the crook of his shoulder, I recall the experience I wrote about in Chapter 14 – The moment outside on my patio on that cold night last January.

"...and God said; *"This will be the last cold winter you ever spend."*

Amen I say. Amen. It was a very cold winter of my life. But even on those cold, damp and dark nights, I managed to keep a fire in the hearth with friendship, family, my writing, and many joyful moments of solitude as kindling for that fire.

CHAPTER 52
PATIENCE IS WORTH PRAYING FOR

Morning Paul Honey:

When you have a few minutes to take a break to read, I'm writing a little bit to you this morning - Just some mornin' thoughts.

One of my young friends is hurting over another breakup. She chooses badly for herself. I thought we'd made some headway, but after arriving late for her visit with me she told me she was late because she had to bring her new boyfriend, who doesn't have a car, to his psychiatrist appointment, then to his probation officer.

At the end of our talk, I asked her to start journaling to me via email her thoughts about why she believes she chooses so poorly. Within a few hours she wrote back and told me that she is scared to death to be alone. This is what I wrote back. After you read my answer to her, I will follow with why I'm sharing this with you.

Angela, you wrote: "I'm scared to death to be alone."

How wonderful that you can see this and admit this. Most people can't, don't or won't.

You know people told me over and over again, I had to be comfortable being alone before the right person would come along. I would say to myself grrrrrrrrrrrrrrrrr................ and how ridiculously paradoxical. I have to enjoy being alone before the right person will come along? Well if I'm enjoying being alone, what's the point of the right person coming along?

But over the last two years, and the last year in particular, I've come to believe this is true. When I'm not comfortable being alone, (and comfortable to me means waiting in joyful anticipation rather than in quiet desperation.) I choose poorly. I choose poorly because in my desire to rush and feel better than I do alone, I don't see and hear the red flags, or rather I see them and hear them, but I turn a deaf ear and blind eye away from them.

So my dear, ahhhhhhhh, yes, I know it sucks...But I do believe like me, your quest is to learn what is so difficult about being WITH yourself, and so unpleasant about being with yourself that you would rather fill your days and nights with someone who is a proven liar and cheat. I know, I know, it sucks.... but the work yields such great rewards. I will help you to do it. I promise. I've already blazed the trail for you.

I can also promise you two things my dear friend:

1. The more you begin to enjoy being with yourself - yes alone, the less frightened you become of being alone for longer periods of time.

2. The less frightened you are of being alone and being single, the more patiently you will wait for the right person to come along.

Right in this moment, the work is to understand why is it so hard to be alone? Let's start there?

One more promise Angie: When you discover that not only can you tolerate being alone, but that you have actually learned to enjoying time alone, even those dry stretches when there is no one on the horizon, can become fertile ground for building self-trust. The more trust you have in yourself, the more resourceful you become in learning to build your own community of friends and develop your own interests.

I met a man on the YMCA tennis courts the other day teaching tennis to people in wheelchairs. I was rounding the walking path and heading toward the courts when I got my first glimpse of him. I was struck instantly by the glowing aura around him as he gently and painstakingly hit the balls to the others.

After standing there for a few minutes mesmerized, and for some unknown reason not at all afraid of his reaction, I walked over to him on one of his breaks and shared my observation of this glowing aura – this energy I saw dancing around him on the court. And probably for the same unknown reason, I was not at all surprised when he gazed directly into my eyes for a long moment, and while smiling the most gentle of smiles, began to share in his thick Cajun accent the secret to his dancing aura.

He shared with me that after 35 years of marriage, and on his 58th birthday his wife left him for a long time friend of theirs, and only one month later he lost his twin brother, "his rock" as he put it, in an accident. He further shared that he spent about two months in deep grief, and though he saw the value in giving himself that time, one morning he woke particularly early to the sound of God speaking to him – actually commanding *him to get off his "derriere," stop feeling sorry for himself, and go help some people who are worse off than he.*

He shared with me that his father taught him that helping people in need is the best way to stop feeling sorry for himself, and that he's glad he listened to both his heavenly and earthly fathers that day. Then he turned his gaze toward the others and said, "Look at them. Look at these precious souls who just wanna'come out and hit some balls on the tennis court like the rest of us. Feel normal again. We all just wanna' feel normal. Don't we cher?"

Tears filled my eyes, and my heart cracked open in a similar way that my breakfast egg did this morning as it rolled off my counter onto the ceramic tile. "Yes sir, I said. We sure do."

Angie, I believe that in this man's reaching out through his own grief to support others, he realized what his father knew years ago, that giving what he himself needed, (love, attention and the opportunity for connection,) was truly the ultimate panacea to the magnified self-focus that often follows loss. I believe that this man has truly earned his own trust in honoring the voice that day that told him to go out and make someone else's.

Yes. Self-trust. That is what learning to enjoy being alone builds, as well as reaching out to others builds (no matter what we might or might not directly get back from them in return.) And when we have earned our own trust Angie, we're no longer rushing to fill the empty space, and we have time to hear the voice of God instructing us. So many great things happen in those empty spaces. That great empty creative void that's teaming with potential. New adventures Angie! Yes, we become truly self-trusting in our own ability to create a happy life. And somewhere along the way, we become our own greatest ally and trusted companion.

It is the work Angie....Self-trust is the mother of all work, and my own losses have clearly illuminated that for me this past year. And in order to earn self-trust, I had to develop more self-love and self-respect. Some of that work was done in community with loving and honest friends, and some in the quiet sometimes glorious, sometimes painful hours alone with myself.

And I'm here for you sweetie. We can learn more about self-trust, self-confidence, self-respect and self-love together.

Namaste, your fellow light chaser ~

Ha Paul honey! I thought I was going to have to explain why I forwarded that letter to you, but I think it's pretty darn self-explanatory. Over the course of the last year, what I wrote in that letter to my friend above has been my work and then my great pleasure. To build a remarkable, fascinating, and enjoyable single life for myself, that balances family, friendships, work, hobbies and interests with wonderful time alone to write and enjoy the pleasure of my own company. As a result, the waiting for an amazing man became easier and easier, and felt less and less urgent. You are proof that my theory works!

CHAPTER 53
CLOCKS TICKING AND SOUP ON THE STOVE
JANUARY 11TH, 2011

Good Morning Handsome,

I wanted you to have something in your inbox when you awoke - A gift perhaps, since you are always giving me gifts and I am not much of a shopper....I reckon the greatest gift I have to give to you is writing to you about how I feel and about who I am at a deeper level.

I was girl talkin' with Sylvia tonight, and telling her about many of the things that I cherish about you. And so I find myself in a place of gratitude. I'm sitting quietly right now. Gabe is still with his dad, and I'm thinking about yesterday afternoon at your lovely Rancho Relaxo. I had this moment with you and the kids that I want to share.

I was at the sink with your precious daughter preparing the bread for dinner, and I looked out the window to see the freezing cold rain. In that moment, I became acutely aware of how warm I felt inside. I was warm and full inside my belly and my heart because I was doing some of the things I love doing most in this entire world.

I was cooking for people I love, I was sharing time with a precious child, bonding, but more importantly just enjoying the pleasure of Victoria's company. I was cozy and warm in a cozy warm home in the dead of the winter. The smell of soup, the laughter of children, and a handsome, loving boyfriend and father milling around at the speed you usually mill with your boundless energy all around me... and I thought to myself, the words that the immortal Louie Armstrong once sang; "What a Wonderful World."... What a Wonderful Moment honey.

Content and continuing to watch the rain fall, I thought about the play "Our Town" and the paragraph in that play that I read over and over and over again that makes me tear up every single time... In the play this little girl has just died, but the angel that has come to take her away to heaven gives her one last minute on earth.

The angel brings her to her kitchen, and this is what she tells the angel:

I can't. I can't go. It goes so fast.. We don't have time to look at one another. She breaks down sobbing...I didn't realize. So all that was going on and we never noticed. Take me back — up the hill — to my grave. But first: Wait! One more look. Good-by, Good-by, world. Good-by, Grover's Corners...Mama and Papa. Good-by to clocks ticking...and Mama's sunflowers. And food and coffee. And new-ironed dresses and hot baths...and sleeping and waking up. Oh, earth, you're too wonderful for anybody to realize you. (III.45-9)

But the earth was not too wonderful for me to realize yesterday. I had that moment that she had after her death, but I was alive to enjoy it. Just a perfect moment in the most ordinary of days, and in an ordinary kitchen... a moment in time that might go otherwise unnoticed if my mind had been busy with my worries or my dreams. But I heard the "clocks ticking" so to speak and the dog moaning and the boys playing and the little girl cooking and the daddy milling and my big open heart beating and full to overflowing with the absolute ineffable pleasure of a perfectly perfect simply ordinary moment.

Those are the moments I live for. When I would sit and pray and envision my love, I wouldn't imagine myself on the French Rivera with him or on an island resort, I would imagine myself cooking soup on a cold Sunday afternoon with he and the kids around me. Gabe of course is there. Matt and Claire are there in my dream as well, but I know that can only be from time to time, since they are busy adults with busy lives of their own now.

So that was my dream, and wow.... I just realized.... just now that my dream came true yesterday. Yes, as I write this last paragraph, know that the realization I am having right now is that I manifested my dream of my perfect day. Yesterday was the dream I dreamed come true.. WOW. I managed to manifest two of my heart's greatest desires – my perfect day, and you!

CHAPTER 54
A Mixed Bag of Nuts

June 18, 2011

It's taken half a century on this planet to make a semblance of peace with my humanity. To come to terms with the fact that many of my spiritual pursuits were so lofty that no human (including my own) could be held to such standards. As a result of this personal peace treaty, I've more fully discovered the pleasures of my own company. I've also made much greater space to enjoy the good company of others. The more love and compassionate I learn to have with myself and with the competing commitments between my flesh and my spirit, the more love and compassionate I have for those around me.

I'm thinking of Paul in particular tonight. Much of the time we're together, Paul and I have a grace and ease - a familiar way of being that feels to me like we've know each other forever. Considering that both of us are very strong willed, self directed, lead, follow, or get out of the way types, we get along reasonably well. Frankly this amazes me, and most of the time when we do disagree, like a Louisiana rain storm, it comes on fast and subsides just as quickly. I feel so grown up in this relationship, and I attribute this feeling to the work I've done this past year.

Case in point: On this particular day we're riding St. Tammany Trace. 28 miles of glorious bike trail on the North Shore of Lake Ponchartrain near New Orleans. We're both hungry, and in the middle of discussing dinner plans we come to a fork in the road. We pause at the fork, and Paul asks me whether I want to take a left to Old Mandeville to eat at the lake or a right to the quaint little town of Abita Springs to eat there. I'm definitive in my response. I say I want to take a right and eat in Abita, and then I veer right onto the trace leaving no room for maybe or perhaps. I see a storm brewing and hear thunder in the background, and having just experienced a tornado with three children in the house last weekend, I want to be close to shelter. He then proceeds to tell me that he would rather take a left and take the longer more forested length of the trace to Mandeville, and explains all the reasons that taking a left is the better choice.

With a touch of PTSD from the weekend before,

still in the throes of my own hormonal storm, and hungry/ cranky like we hypoglycemic folks with an empty belly are prone to get, I slam on my bike breaks and come to a screeching halt, (literally screeching) whip my head around like the demon child in the Exorcist, and shout; "DON'T PRETEND TO GIVE ME A CHOICE IF I REALLY DON'T HAVE ONE." And then I launch into a tirade about how much I despise being manipulated into believing someone cares about my preference when they really don't, and how people like to take those 50/50 odds that I would go with their choice, and then they would end up cleverly having me believe that it was my decision all along.

At one point he rode ahead of me to get away from my ranting, and I in turn, slowed down to widen the gap. But after a couple of minutes of fighting the urge to pivot back down the trail, hop in my car and drive back to Baton Rouge, I remembered a promise I made to him about not leaving when I'm upset. I called up to him to slow down instead. In the time it took us both to bridge the gap, me speeding up and him slowing down, he had reached into his backpack and found a bag of nuts he keeps just for such occasions. Extending the bag toward me, he lovingly urged; "Hungry Honey? Want some of these mixed nuts?"

Still peddling fast as a mallard and hot as a Cajun Gumbo, I cut him a cross look. Like an adolescent in a hissy fit, I snatch the bag out of his hands and retort in a snarky manner; "Don't think just because I'm hungry or hormonal, I don't have a legitimate complaint here."...Thank heavens that my good sense was able to lure the hungry and hormonal middle-aged adolescent back in with a bribe of nuts and make her swallow a big portion before she spoke again.

Belly full of nuts, and a few long moments later my sensibilities return. I rode for two or three minutes more on the expensive, and much appreciated sparkling champagne colored bike he gave me on one of our very first biking adventures on The Trace. Silent and reflective, I eventually began to slow my pace down.

Shortly after, I found myself shaking my head from side to side, laughing out loud, and saying in the most apologetic voice my ego would allow; "I still don't like being given a fake choice, but I'm OK going left to the lake." This time I give him a moment to explain his choice to go left, and he tells me he wanted to drop something off to his young daughter. Ahhhh...a moment to connect with his precious little lass on a day that the court says is not his to have her. Now understood.

I instantly feel compassion for both Paul and myself for wanting to snatch those precious moments with our young whenever we can get them. Fortunately, and to both Ryan's credit and my own, we've been very generous and gracious with spontaneous visitations by the other parent and have both managed to keep the impersonal "family court" system out of our very personal affairs. Paul however, despite his best efforts, is not so fortunate.

I'm overwhelmed in that moment with the realization that a judge person (an employee of the state of Louisiana, who has never spent one minute watching he and his children interact,) is making decisions that will greatly affect his relationship with them. So I reach out, extend my right hand to hold his left, and true to his nature, he graciously accepted it as we rode in tandem for the remaining six miles to the lake. We chat, enjoy the scenery and the pleasure of each other's company. I feel gratitude on this ride for his and my own ability to "get off it" quickly. I feel gratitude for his compassion and understanding of both my mid-life hormonal surges and my ravenous rants that ambush me in the middle of an otherwise lovely outing – making mountains out of mole hills, making minor skirmishes seem like hills worth dying on.

I'm reminded of a conversation I once had with a beautiful friend with an equally beautiful name, "Chanler." We were discussing her enviable relationship with her husband. It's of both great personal and professional interest of mine to observe couples who have what I consider exceptional relationships. I ask lots of questions about what makes them work, and I watch them at play.

So we were talking about what makes their marriage work, when she shared that in all the years they've been married, they've never gone to bed angry. When I asked her what her secret was, she said; "I'm not quite sure, but what I do know is that when we start to fight, within a couple of sentences, one of us realizes we'd rather be happy than right, and we let it go.

I remember thinking that day that I wanted a relationship like that. I wanted my beloved and I to be way more committed to each other's happiness, and to the health of our relationship than to either of our egos. And what I've noticed in my 20 years as a marriage counselor is that when the primary allegiance is to one's ego, the goodwill along with the marriage erodes. However, when the primary allegiance is to the relationship, the relationship thrives.

With my blood sugar back to normal now, I'm able to remember I have that now with Paul. I get that he wants that with me, and it was our allegiance to the relationship that had him slow down and me speed up to re-connect within a matter of minutes rather than days.

Another wave of appreciation washes over me, and still biking hand in hand, I'm aware of how steady he is in life's small and big storms. He is strong willed, yes, but he is even tempered too. Ahhhh, that fairly agreeable Alpha I spoke of earlier. Yes, I'm full again, and not just from Paul's mixed bag of nuts. I'm full because I trust this man to stay steady in my hormonal storms, as well and life's unpredictable everyday storms that tend to ambush us on an otherwise ordinary, going well day. I also trust him to weather the big storms, because I've heard his stories of Katrina and how he stoically managed and cared for his family through the flooding and destruction of their home.

He left footprints, as he likes to say, on the bottom of the ocean, so I'm clear he can handle my hunger as well as my mid-life moments. Yes, I trust this man, and I trust this relationship. And though it is too soon for me to predict whether he will ultimately be "the one," I do know that at this juncture I adore him and our relationship, because somewhere along this Blue Moon journey, I learned to adore myself.

THE END

AFTERWORD
THE MIRACLES OF MAY

EXCERPT FROM CHAPTER 12:

He is honest and has great integrity. He is a professional and is well established in his career. He is ambitious, industrious in his career and loves what he does. He is alpha, virile, athletic, poised, and strong. He is beautiful inside and out...

At the beginning of May 2011, and in preparation for a workshop I was to give that weekend on managing anxiety, I remembered that in my red journal was a quote from my mentor Charlie that I wanted to share and discuss. So I tumbled into bed exhausted (which was not unusual those days,) reached across to the top of my nightstand and grabbed my red velvet journal with the rhinestone heart on the front.

As I began to search the pages for the quote, I noticed toward the middle, a very bright multi-colored set of pages. At first I stared at the pages not remembering having written them - fogginess and forgetfulness have played a sizable role in this menopausal mini-series. But upon closer examination, the experience of having written them as well as writing about them in Chapter 12 came back to me.

Once again in rainbow print was the narrative of what I wanted in a man. The narrative that I had written upon completing the book *The Soulmate Secret*.

It's important to note that I found this list again in early May. May - the time of year the card spread that Sylvia read for me predicted my prayers would be answered. I had forgotten about that too. Early May was also a moment in my life where I was feeling uncertain about whether to continue my relationship with Paul. I had recently been diagnosed with Mono (yes, the kissing disease) and the 85 mile dating commute back and forth to the North Shore of New Orleans was beyond exhausting as well.

I discovered the mono after having finally surrendered my one woman battle with menopause. I had finally tapping out of my self-designed research project and surrendered to a holistic practitioner who specialized in nutrition based menopausal relief. In an effort to ease the burden of my hormonal deficits and fluctuations, and having run all the appropriate blood tests, she did indeed find my hormones seriously out of balance, (though my children, my office manager and my boyfriend could have told her this.) She also found in my blood work the Ebstein Barr (mono) virus running ramped in my system. So I was walloped with a double whammy of mono and menopause and as a result feeling overwhelmed, fatigued and uncertain as to whether to continue the stress of a new relationship that added further to the imbalance of it all.

I shared my feelings over the course of the last week of April and first week of May with Paul. We had some very impassioned discussions. Including but not limited to, Paul considering moving onto the same street as his ex-wife in a house that came up for sale in the last several weeks. After a day long discussion about the possibility of cooling the flames between us, Paul compassionately sent me some research he had done on Mono. He had highlighted one symptom of mono in particular that said; *"Relationships can be strained, and sometimes feel impossible to maintain during the course of this illness."* This man clearly did not want to lose me.

So on that fateful night in May, climbing into bed, still feeling great exhaustion, still feeling uncertain as to whether I had energy for a relationship, and preparing for my workshop on anxiety management (we do teach what we need to learn,) I notice my rainbow list of man qualities that I had written last fall and noted earlier in this book. As I read down the narrative of characteristics, my eyes began to fill, a lump formed in my throat ,and I began to weep. Paul had most of the qualities that I had written in those three pages.

Yes, it was a tall, tall order, as I wrote on the bottom of that list and referenced in a passage of Chapter 12. And yet Paul, with a few exceptions, was able to fill it beautifully. And as Claire once shared with me about her beloved, God was generous enough to add a few other qualities that I didn't even know to ask for. I closed the book, and called my amazing man. I shared with him my discovery, and we pledged to each other I would get through both menopause and mono with his support.

He decided against the house, thank God, and he not only accompanied me on my next visit to the holistic bio-identical hormone specialist, but he paid for the entire visit, plus the plethora of vitamins and nutritional supplements, like soy nuts and whey protein shakes. He calls this an investment in our future. True to his consistent nature, he kept his pledge to help me through this tough, tough time.

So Six months later, I'm happy to report that both the symptoms of mono and menopause have been relieved. They've been relieved with Paul's patient, loving support and my own personal pledge to continued psycho/spiritual growth and great health. In lieu of taking traditional medicines, I opted for natural supplements. I'm happy to report the fog has lifted on my mind and my mood, and my overwhelm has been downgraded to manageable anxiety. The workshop, by the way, went exceptionally well, since my current life, once again, had prepared me to speak from my heart and my own recent experience.

And the paradox of wanting the security of June Cleaver's life as well as great adventure? Well at least at this passage; I have it with Paul. Paul has more energy than many people combined, and like my pirate ancestors, he's a hearty seaman as well as an adventurer on land. In the months we've been together we've set sail on many adventures and together continue to discover new and endless pleasures.

I met with paradox, and paradox showed me how to expand - to bridge the gap between things I could not reconcile.

And it's worth stating here that I'm no longer an idealistic school girl. I'm a seasoned professional, and I fully appreciate that the relationship is still green and tender and we both have school aged children to blend and thus the future uncertain. (Then again, when exactly is anyone's future truly certain?) But when giving advice on relationship decisions, I've always said a couple should weather four seasons, one crisis or natural disaster and a long road trip before they make any long term commitments.

We've made it through the health crisis, and one middle-sized road trip quite successfully. Fall, winter and spring are also behind us as we head into a longer road trip to New York and the heat of mid-summer. And like our rides on the trace, they'll be other forks in the road to negotiate, and rivers to cross, and I'll continue to look for the sign posts along the way to help me navigate into the future. No matter what Paul and I ultimately decide, I feel promise, expectancy and great adventure ahead, and for now I'm happy with the path I'm following and in no rush to get anywhere but here and now — fully engaged in the wonders of this present moment.

With respect to the card "YOUR PRAYERS HAVE

BEEN ANSWERED" – the card that Sylvia pulled last fall – the one that foretold what would happen in May of this year, the one that I wrote about in Chapter 40 and said: *I have no clear concept of what might happen next May. May of 2011. But I've come to trust the cards.* Yes, I really had no way of predicting what would happen this May. But I had faith something wonderful would.

As I see it, the Miracles of May revealed themselves to me in an enfoldment of three layers:

1. Via May's re-discovery of my rainbow narrative of qualities that I had implored the Universe to deliver for me. And deliver it did, by way of a beautiful, soulful, loving man named Paul. (And to think now that in my great physical and emotional fatigue of late April, I was close to tossing this wonderful man back into the sea or "gulf" as the case may be.)

2. In the miraculous timing of being shown (in full color I might add,) that Paul had many of the qualities I was looking for in a beloved. Though weary to the bone, discovering that narrative on that fateful night, enabled me to reach in and simultaneously

reach out further to him and ask for and receive the support I needed to fully recover.

3. May also marked the beginning of my restoration process, the restoration of the structural integrity of my endocrine system, and as a result the simultaneous restoring of my energy and enthusiasm for life which had been greatly compromised in the spring of this year.

Though the debilitating symptoms of mono are now behind me, I'm still adhering to the new found rituals of twenty minute "safety naps" (as Paul endearingly refers to them) and I'm still working less hours, and learning to let my body say NO, even when my spirit wants to say YES. As a matter of fact, even when the mono and menopause completely subside, I've decided I'm going to keep my safety naps, continue to work less, and keep my new found ability to say "NO" as three new enlightened self-interest rituals.

Through this years trials and triumphs, I've come to see more clearly that life is full of many delicious and sometimes distasteful surprises. And it's totally up to us to decide whether to make life's lemons into lemonade. It's always our choice. Yes, I believe that it's our divine birth right to compose and play our own life symphonies - the opening sonata all the way through to the final allegro.

As far as my love hate relationship with Paradox - that great debate between freewill and destiny? I had a friend once share his philosophy with me, and I now believe it to be true. He said that life is like a college curriculum. Some of the courses are required (meeting my ex-husband, and Ryan, having our children, and getting a divorce) and some of the courses are electives (the learnings that took place in those experiences.)

I believe I've become softer, more pliable and expanded as a result of my life's challenges, simply because I made a conscious choice to do so. I also believe I could have chosen to harden, close off and turn bitter had that been my intention instead.

And with all the above said, I already know if another Blue Moon rises, I'll be risin' with it. This year's mid-life adventures have taught me just that. They've taught me self-trust and a deeper way to love.

ACKNOWLEDGMENTS

As Einstein once said; If I have seen further it is only by standing on the shoulders of giants. So how could I possible begin to share my gratitude for everyone who contributed in their own unique way to the understanding and consciousness I have developed over the course of writing and publishing this memoir? So many of my dearest companions have made it into the fabric of this book by way of the contribution you are to my life. You will know who you are by the loving way in which I speak of you.

Matthew, Claire and Gabriel, My deepest appreciation goes to my cherished offspring. Having worked hard to encourage you to forge your own authentic paths, I am absolutely mesmerized at the beautiful tapestry you have woven in designing your lives. I am continually inspired by the three of you.

Paul, I dreamed you, and you came true. You have this precious gift of looking beyond your own needs for ways to make my life and other's lives more joyful. Thank you for your exceptional love and daily acts of kindness, and supporting me through a health crisis that at times must have made those menopausal moments seem like days.

Faith, my dear daily companion and office manager extraordinaire, I meant it when I warned you, when you leave I'm going to cut grass on the neutral ground of I-10. You are my own Radar O'Reilly. You dedication and warmth and skill make anyone (including me) who crosses the threshold of the office feel important and worth the trouble you take. I deeply appreciate your encouragement and support throughout the writing and editing of this book.

Sidney, my late father, you taught me to appreciate the good earth and to appreciate the company of others. Your love for life was contagious. You taught me to love horses, and the bayou, baby gators and baby "anythings" that found their way from the swamp to our farm needing care. You taught me to love the hum of a tractor, and the setting sun and the rising sound of crickets and frogs announcing the night. You taught me to be kind to strangers and generous with those less fortunate. You taught me that dry humor makes a day more joyful and a crisis more manageable, and that evening time was for watching the education channel and connecting with those we love.

Mother, ever important to the fabric of this book was the grace and beauty of your own middle years. I have dedicated this book to you.

Cody, thank you for being the kind of person I can trust 100% in editing my book and helping me through my resistance to the electronic age of publishing. You have great integrity as a journalist and as a man, and I am deeply blessed to have you on my dream team. You WILL have an extraordinary career in journalism. I already know this.

Brent, my god-son, I will forever remember the time we shared together in creating that magnificent masterpiece destined to become the front cover of this book. I still have a clear image of the morning I walked into my office, blues blaring in the background, your paint brush and full attention to the canvas, and seeing you clearly in your bliss. Priceless.

My Wednesday group and my Integral group, I would not and could not have written this book from the depths of self-understanding without your honesty, love, commitment and dedication to being deep divers yourselves.

Andy, Beverly, Debra, Melinda and Sylvia, My deep appreciation to each of you for your feedback on the manuscript. Your keen eyes and your honest hearts gave me the strength and courage to go the last nine yards.

Chanler, I was both honored and thrilled to have you accept my offer to be a part of my book "Sangha." Your Flippy books are among my most cherished possessions, and I read them often to my young ones. Your talents are many and I am blessed to have you share them with me. I cried when I woke up to find your designs for the cover waiting patiently in my morning email. They were even more stunning than I imagined.

Vince, thank you for the extraordinary photos for the back cover. You are a man of many talents, as you managed to get great pictures in the short window of time Mother Nature gave us on the Mississippi Delta that morning. Know that for many reasons you are among my most cherished friends.

Arielle Ford and Liz Gilbert – Both *The Soulmate Secret* and *Eat Pray Love* were given to me in perfect and divine timing by women who wanted for my great happiness. My deep gratitude to the two of you for having the courage to share your own journey, which in turn inspired me to share mine. I could only hope to leave a fraction of the imprint on others that you have left on me. My life will never be the same after having been allowed a window into yours. Again, If I have seen further it is only by standing on the shoulders of giants.

CPSIA information can be obtained at www.ICGtesting.com
Printed in the USA
LVOW081024030112

262159LV00006B/10/P